FACING THE CHALLENGES OF SOCIAL WORK IN AUSTRALIAN RURAL AND REMOTE COMMUNITIES

Lesley Chenoweth and Daniela Stehlik

FACING THE CHALLENGES OF SOCIAL WORK IN AUSTRALIAN RURAL AND REMOTE COMMUNITIES

Juggling the Demands of Practice

Social Work
Collection Editor
Kate Parkinson

LPP

First published in 2025 by Lived Places Publishing

British Library Cataloguing in Publication Data
A CIP record for this book is available from the British Library.

ISBN: 9781917503969 (pbk)
ISBN: 9781917503983 (ePDF)
ISBN: 9781917503976 (ePUB)

Cover design by Fiachra McCarthy
Book design by Rachel Trolove of Twin Trail Design
Typeset by Newgen Publishing, UK

Lived Places Publishing
P.O. Box 1845
47 Echo Avenue
Miller Place, NY 11764

www.livedplacespublishing.com

Acknowledgements

We acknowledge the traditional custodians of the lands and waters on which we live and work: the Yuggera and Turrbul people in Queensland and the Ngunnawal people in the ACT. We recognise their enduring connection to the land, seas, and waterways which have always been places of community and culture, and pay our respect to them, their elders past and present, and to their cultures.

We take this opportunity to offer our sincere thanks to our many colleagues who worked with us over many years and in many places across Australia. To Donna, Flo, Clare, Paula, Matthew, and many others, it is through these collaborations and friendships that we all gained a deeper understanding of what life and work in rural and remote settings are really like and how social workers can be better supported in their practice.

To the many respondents who gave their time and shared their experiences so unreservedly, we remain grateful for your honesty and generosity in bringing your communities to real life. We are in awe of your advocacy as the backbone of your communities.

These are important stories. Social workers and students everywhere, we see you! We might run into you on the track somewhere.

Abstract

Living and working in rural and remote communities brings a range of different experiences for their residents. Isolation, distance from major centres, and limited access to health and other services bring challenges, while close-knit community connections and shared identity in place can be a strength. Social workers also experience these challenges and strengths. Rural practice requires being an effective ethical practitioner as well as being part of the community and place. This book brings together several decades of our experiences working in rural and remote Australian communities and listening to stories of lived experience from residents and practitioners. We offer an increased confidence in a community-focused practice that strengthens the resilience of both community members and those working alongside them.

Key words

Rural social work, communities, place and identity, resilience, strengths-based practice, community practice, ethic of flourishing, practice frameworks

Contents

Acronyms

AASW	Australian Association of Social Workers
ABS	Australian Bureau of Statistics
AIFS	Australian Institute of Family Studies
AIHW	Australian Institute of Health and Welfare
CASW	Canadian Association of Social Workers
CBD	Central business district
CoP	Communities of Practice
COVID-19	Coronavirus disease of 2019
CRC	Cooperative Research Centre
DiDo	Drive in Drive out
ESW	Environmental Social Work
FiFo	Fly in Fly out
FNQ	Far North Queensland
GDP	Gross Domestic Product
GP	General Practitioner
GSW	Green Social Work
IFSW	International Federation of Social Work
Kms	Kilometres
LAC	Local Area Coordination
LACs	Local Area Coordinators
LGA	Local Government Association
NASW	National Association of Social Workers (US)
NDIS	National Disability Insurance Scheme
NFCRC	Nuclear Fuel Cycle Royal Commission
NFP	Not-for-profit

NGO	Non-Government Organisation
NIMBY	Not in my backyard
NRMB	Natural Resources Management Board
NSW	New South Wales
NT	Northern Territory
QCOSS	Queensland Council of Social Services
Qld	Queensland
PO	Professional Officer (Qld Government)
RFDS	Royal Flying Doctor Service
SBA	Strengths Based Approach
SBP	Strengths Based Practice
UK	United Kingdom
US	United States
WA	Western Australia
WiFi	Wireless Fidelity
WW2	World War Two

1
Rural Australia: Its places, spaces and people

Learning objectives

- Identify features of Australia: its geography and demography
- Describe key concepts that are central to this book
- Reflect on how the rural impacts on social work practice

1 Welcome

Congratulations on finding and opening this book about being a rural social work practitioner.

We have designed this book to assist you in your studies, as well as to broaden your understanding of how practice outside of cities and urban settings can be both challenging and rewarding. However, as we propose to explain here, it has different characteristics.

Social work as a discipline had its early genesis in the late nineteenth and early twentieth centuries in cities, as a response to ongoing industrialisation. As long ago as 1993, Canadian Ken Collier asked whether 'social work methods and theories [could] be transferred successfully from the urban context, where they were first developed, to rural regions?' (1993, p. 3). We agree with Collier that they can be, so long as we are aware of their differences, the implications of the politics of place, and make the most of the opportunities they offer.

We are pleased to present a focus on rural and remote practice from the perspective of the practitioner, you. We draw on our now several decades of experience in teaching, researching, evaluating, and advocating for social workers in several states of Australia.

While such rural social work practice has a history, which we touch on briefly in the next chapter, it is also a dynamic present-day reality that gives each practitioner a stimulating environment in which to work.

We particularly describe how place enables a deep knowledge of the strengths, resources, and challenges of these communities. Drawing on our experiences, we suggest just how the rural and remote practitioner can positively contribute to their local communities, and, in particular, how this can be done in both an ethical and professional manner.

This introduction will explain how we gathered the evidence of the lived experiences that we draw on here and how these also link to our own journey in practice. This chapter also gives an explanation of the definitions we use and the meanings of key terms such as 'rural' and 'remote', as well as others, which will guide your reading in subsequent chapters. At the end of each chapter, we offer some reflective questions. To encourage you to read further and in more depth, we have also gathered together a significant reference list, which you will find at the end of the book. This gives further resources from our own research, as well as others.

We will discuss in more detail the ties that bind us to place in Chapter 4 and in Chapter 3, we explain the difference between ties of kin and blood and ties of association as regards community.

Here, as part of this brief introduction, it is important to note that we consider the ties that bind us to 'the rural' in this present day are likely to be by association. What do we mean by this? Attachment through some form of association, and most commonly this will be through work.

Historically, the ties that bound European Australians to the rural were most likely through kinship networks. It was once a truism that everyone in the city had a relative of some kind in the country. This relationship truism came to mean that everyone just 'understood' the rural because it was connected to us by kin and blood. For example, Lesley can trace her family origins back to the early nineteenth century and their settlement in a rural region. However, most commonly, this is no longer the case. As the post-WW2 migration boom strengthened, those who arrived in Australia (such as Daniela's parents) did not have that connection; and this is increasingly so as that migration has continued over the past decades.

As a result, if we consider our connections to the rural today, it will be through our work-related networks. This seems a good opportunity to also make the point stronger by highlighting that while a historical experience of place tends to inform present-day policymakers and politicians, they are unlikely to be born and raised rurally (although we have some exceptions), and given their career paths, are unlikely, in many cases, to have even visited remote locations. If they do visit as part of their work association, they are likely to be 'on the ground' for a minimum amount of time, meet a few carefully selected individuals, and then return to the city. In this way, their assumptions about place, community, and the rural/remote landscape more broadly are powerfully shaped by these brief connections. For example, a policymaker in the city making a decision looks at the map and chooses a location for an aged care home that may be more than 200 km from a rural town where people live, making regular contact with their family more difficult.

It is important at the very outset that, as you read this book, you are aware that we are not seeking a utopian ideal, nor are we asking you, the practitioner, to make it your career to do so. We are asking you to consider working in rural or remote communities, and to do so with as much of a clear appreciation of the historical, ideological, and pragmatic context as you can. This book raises a number of critical issues that you will confront in your practice. Chapters 5 and 6 provide you with some resources to assist you in your practice. We also have spent some time explaining how rural practice 'works' and how, as a practitioner, you can celebrate what may appear to be small achievements, but what are, in fact, important milestones. Through a mobilisation of community, through the creation of networks and alliances, we argue that there are ways in which you can make a difference. We do not subscribe to the view that social work is a 'vocation' or a 'calling'. Instead, we suggest social work, as a values-based profession with an extensive knowledge base and skills, can positively contribute to rural communities and those who live there.

The chapter now begins with a brief outline of the rural within an Australian context, the people, and the challenges and opportunities that they face.

2 The 'rural' in an Australian context: Myths and realities

With its history of human settlement of some 65,000 years, Australia has the world's longest surviving continuous Indigenous culture. This was dramatically changed in the late eighteenth century, with the arrival of European colonisation and settlement. The eastern coastline of Australia first became a penal colony to alleviate overcrowded British prisons, with later free settlers seeking opportunities for better lives and prosperity. As these settlers began to farm, the indigenous landscape was changed irrevocably.

We should note here that the early pioneers farmed as if they were still located in Europe, with its rich soils and milder climate. In doing so, they ignored the deep appreciation of the land held by its First Nations inhabitants, and this, associated with the many attempts by those inhabitants to challenge the newcomers, resulted in massacres, many of which are only now becoming known and recognised. For those of you interested in reading about this painful history, which continues to shape and impact how we 'deliver' human services, there are some outstanding texts available. For example, Bruce Pascoe's 'Dark Emu,' released in 2014 (Pascoe, 2014), had a powerful effect on its Australian readership. Another publication by Bill Gammage, 'The Biggest Estate on Earth: How Aborigines Made Australia,' published in 2011 is also highly recommended (Gammage, 2011)

To return now to our brief chronology. A major gold rush in the mid-nineteenth century resulted in considerable in-migration, not only of European, but also of Asian and North American settlers. For the First Nations people, this continued colonisation and its radical changes to lifestyle were to prove destructive to their long-held relationships with their landscapes and to their health and wellbeing, as they were forced further and further inland, away from their traditional homelands: a historic pattern that can be seen to be repeated in many other colonised nations during this time, including in the Americas and Africa.

Australia was federated in 1901 and for around the 60 years following this, it was largely underpinned economically by primary production: wheat, sheep, cattle, and other forms of agriculture. We were then proud to be a primary producing nation in feeding ourselves and the rest of the world. During this time, 'the rural' was lauded and even mythologised, as much of our early literature and art highlights.

This early colonisation history, and its foundation in what has been termed a 'theft' of land from its original inhabitants, has shaped the cultural consciousness in the present day. To many of us, 'the bush' continues to evoke a natural, pristine, and essentially good place that, while it may be less than the city we live in, is still morally our national conscience. We respond emotionally to the ideology of the pioneering spirit, the challenge against the unknown as essentially the concept of 'the rural' (Lockie

& Bourke, 2001). When asked, for example, to describe a 'typi-cal Australian,' we respond with stereotypes, such as Crocodile Dundee, that revert to masculine interpretations. Despite this, most of us continue to live on the eastern seaboard and know little or nothing about the lives of those people whom we mythologise. The reality of family life in rural Australia, the lives of women and children (as well as men) in that environment, is less well understood. The mythic persona of the Australian as the tamer of 'wide open spaces' and of 'bronzed Aussies' col-onising the inland with a pioneering spirit and a determined individualism tied up with 'mateship' and giving everyone a 'fair go' was well established over 100 years ago and remains essen-tially potent. One way we can better understand such power-ful imagery is to think about the stereotypes that continue to shape 'the rural' in Australia.

Stereotypes can be understood as attributes we assign so that we can 'classify' people. What is important here is that such stere-otypes can often lead to prejudices, which in turn tend to prevail as attitudes that can demean, thereby leading to discrimination. These stereotypes are continually rehearsed in all forms of media (including social media), to the point that we are often, albeit unconsciously, influenced by them. How does this impact the social work practitioner? In two ways – the first, the stereotypes associated with their clients and their communities; the second, the stereotypes associated with them as practitioners work-ing in these environments. We return to this in further detail in Chapter 4.

As urbanisation accelerated, the city became more central to the nation's identity, and now, if we consider the rural in Australia, our thoughts also turn to the environment, to climate change impacts, to resource extraction, to tourism, not just to agriculture. Nevertheless, we argue here that enduring stereotypes continue to cast a long shadow in rural and remote Australia by suggesting that those who choose to live outside our cities are conservative, traditional, patriarchal, and intolerant of difference.

Our work spans almost three decades, but we still find that these stereotypes continue to re-emerge and linger. Why? As we mentioned above, stereotyping leads to prejudice, both positive and negative. Importantly, human beings tend to define themselves and their sense of identity by who they are not. Practitioners will find very quickly how a sense of identity associated with place defines their clientele and their communities as well as themselves.

Over the past century, as the city became the place to be and to work, the rural declined in attractiveness. It was less a desirable place to work; people there were 'slightly weird', and being 'sent to the country' was seen as something less than career enhancing. It follows then that working in a rural setting, whether as a nurse, a teacher, a police officer, or a social worker, was to be avoided. Those who did identify with the rural or who avoided cities and deliberately moved to the countryside were viewed as perhaps contributing much less to the great national endeavor. We return to this paradox further in later chapters.

However, we stress here that the historically powerful image of Rural Australia (capital letters) as a place only connected with agriculture continues to shape our national thinking about places other than those we can consider urban. This also tends to ignore the lived reality of those First Nations people as displaced and living largely in the central and northern parts of the country. This by no means implies that Indigenous Australians do not live in cities, but the concept of 'rural' as an imaginary tends to elide any others than those associated with agriculture. One of the many ways in which this historical, but essentially mythological ideology has continued to be challenged is through the increasing demands for land rights by Indigenous Australians. Indigenous people constitute a higher proportion of rural, and especially remote, populations of Australia. Most recently, the relationship between Indigenous Australians (both Aboriginal and Torres Strait Islander peoples) and the land has become the subject of both academic and popular discourse. One way in which this has entered into the national consciousness is through the increasing use of the names given by traditional owners to the land on which we live and work.

3 A 'tyranny' of distance and demography

We use the word 'tyranny' here as it has become a powerful and well-understood term associated with the large expanse of the Australian continent. This creates ongoing challenges of providing services to small, discrete geographic communities that have little infrastructure and are dispersed by large distances from urban centres. Interestingly, the concept itself was first coined by an American geographer, William Bunge, and subsequently taken up in Australia in the early 1960s. It has now become a 'shorthand' way of explaining why living outside cities results in recognition of few supports for individuals (Wedesweiler, 2025

https://www.sbs.com.au/news/article/second-class-citizens-
the-grim-reality-of-avoidable-deaths-in-regional-australia/s5cyls
kf8 Accessed: 22nd February 2025).

So just how big is Australia? The continent can be crossed from east to west (a distance of some 3,290 kms) by car in about 41 hours, or by plane in just over 4 hours. Western Standard Time means that Perth is 3 hours 'behind' Sydney, a factor that impacts much service delivery decision-making in that state. From south to north (just over 3,000 kms) will take around 31 hours by car, and by plane just over 3 hours. If there is a stop-over to the north at Alice Springs (roughly halfway), the plane journey will take just over 6 hours. The continent consists of some 7.6 m. sq. kilo-metres, being just slightly smaller than the US at about 8 m. sq. kms. Queensland has a population of 4.6 m. spread over an area of 1.7 m. sq. kms, which is nearly seven times larger than the British Isles and larger than South Africa.

The roads between these major centres are highways, most often two lanes, and kept in a reasonable condition. A major stretch of the Eyre Highway between Western Australia and north-western South Australia was only finally sealed in 1976. Until then, it was a dirt road, a muddy quagmire in winter, and a dusty stretch in summer: an adventure to drive, to say the least. In some places, such as in Far North Queensland (FNQ), some roads are pur-posely left unsealed because of the regular monsoonal flooding that occurs.

The population of Australia is skewed to its coastline and to urban centres. Over 69 per cent of us live in our major cities. The Australian Institute of Family Studies (AIFS) estimates that around 20 per cent of the population live in 'inner' regional centres; 9 percent in outer regional areas, and 2.3 per cent in remote or very remote areas (1.5 percent remote and 0.8 per cent very remote). Of the total population of First Nations people, 14.4 per cent or 150,900 people, live in remote or very remote areas. There are also scattered geographic communities in Western Australia, Queensland, and the Northern Territory that are First Nations populated only (more detail can be found at: Australian Institute of Family Studies https://aifs.gov.au/research/facts-and-figures/families-and-family-composition Accessed: 3rd December 2024).

The AIFS suggests 'remote' as being determined by the road distance from services. It also makes the point that very little 'is known about families living in rural and remote areas ... compared to those living in major cities' (Baxter, 2011, p. 1). The classification 'remoteness' is officially measured by governments as the physical distance by road to the nearest urban centre and accordingly underpins policies and programs. Some 60 per cent of the nation's mining is operated in remote Australia. In 2012, mining contributed 8.4 per cent of our GDP (Gross Domestic Product) and accounted for 55 per cent of our export GDP. In addition, mining employs some 240,000 people across Australia; however, not all of these people live in remote geographic communities. Remote Australia is also home to nearly half of Australia's GDP in agriculture (4 per cent) and to over 40,000 small to medium enterprises, one and a half times more per capita than the national average (CRC for Remote Economic Participation, 2012).

Some of the major policy decisions that impact First Nations Australians are those who live rurally and remotely. This is very much about place. As this rural and remote population lives in small communities and settlements scattered across the northern and western part of the country, they continue to be 'managed' centrally, either from Canberra, our capital city in which the Federal government has most of its public service departments, or a little more closely by state governments from the state capital cities. Place becomes identified strongly with its inhabitants, and, as we describe in more detail in Chapter 4, place becomes synonymous, positively or negatively, with those inhabitants. In some extreme cases, a place is known by shorthand; no more needs saying, as this shorthand identifies the vulnerable 'clientele'. The concern here is that such labeling adds further to derogatory connotations of the people who live there.

Our major cities are all on the coast, as are many of the regional centres. The three states in which we conducted our research (Queensland, Western Australia, and the Northern Territory) together make up about 73 per cent of the total land area, with roughly 30 per cent of the population. These states together include nearly 50 per cent of our First Nations population. (For more detail see Australian Bureau of Statistics at www.abs.gov. au). A quick example of the 'tyranny' argument can be given from Western Australia, where over 75 per cent of the population of 1.97 m live in the capital city, Perth, or in its immediate metropolitan area. It takes some 22 hours by car to drive from Perth to Broome in the far north of the state, or just over two and a half hours by plane. The north-west of the state, which includes the region of the Kimberley (from Perth 2,545 kms.), takes 29 hours to reach by car. The population of this area in June 2023 was just under 40,000, of which some 14,400 (around 36 per cent) identified as First Nations. Most Australians would agree that the

Kimberley is considered 'remote'. A quick check shows it can take up to 16 hours, at prohibitive expense, to fly from Sydney (via Perth) to Kununurra, the major centre in the area.

Remote Australia often makes the metropolitan headlines because of housing costs. Not that long ago, it was because regional councils were offering houses for as little as AUD$1.00 if people would just come and live there and renovate. At the time of writing this, the headlines report that rental properties in some centres, such as Karratha and Port Hedland, in north-west Western Australia, can cost well over AUD$1,000 per week. Overnight stays in motels can cost the equivalent of the capital city CBD and are often booked out by 'cashed-up' mining personnel.

These costs have a domino effect, as governments scramble to build new housing stock, while human service agencies have difficulty in recruiting and retaining staff. As we write this, Port Hedland mayor Peter Carter has just been quoted as saying that '… fresh housing was needed to attract government workers [as] governments haven't invested money in housing in a long, long time. I think they realise now if you want teachers and police to come to regional areas, you must have good housing, because they won't live in a house that's 40 years old' (Kordic, Shakleton & Bidstrup, 2025).

Delivering essential health, education, and human services in rural and remote communities has been historically, and continues to remain, a critical challenge for Australia. In the past two decades, there has been a change in the quality of life for many people living in rural communities as a result of recent social and economic disadvantage. This has emerged as a result of falling commodity prices, globalisation of markets, climate change (particularly drought), and out-migration of population to metropolitan areas (Stehlik, 2001, 2013). At the same time, the service responses to rural communities have also changed with a resultant loss of social capital (Winter, 2000). In the mid-1990s, the then federal government withdrew a number of key services from rural areas, including important services associated with caring for a family member. More recently, there have been attempts to 're-instate' such services by using different models of care support (Chenoweth & Stehlik, 1999). However, it takes time to rebuild such infrastructure and to ensure that these services are adequately staffed. For example, it has been calculated that there is one nurse for 170 people in remote Australia, compared with one nurse for every 100 people in metropolitan Australia. A recent media report cited the following:

> While living in a remote area can be incredibly rewarding sometimes, the need for services for our children can make the isolation frustrating and challenging. Did you know the average wait time for a speech pathologist in remote Australia is up to four years? (Remote Australians Matter, 2024).

A recent newspaper article was headed 'A dire warning amid rural Queensland healthcare exodus' as the struggle to recruit and retain professionals continues (Simmerton, 2025). We discuss strategies that have been developed to cope with these statistics further in Chapter 5.

As a brief comparison, a recent United States report has identified that 1/5th (around 50 m.) of the population live in areas classified as non-urban. The report highlights that these have lower incomes, less access to employer-sponsored health insurance, worse health outcomes, and have, over the past decade, experienced the closure of many of their local hospitals, particularly their maternity hospitals (Alker, Osorio & Edgar, 2025). See also Rickertts (2005) with respect to health workforce in rural areas.

Other consequences of the impact of change in rural Australia have been the diminution of volunteer effort, the fragmentation of extended families, the ageing of the population, and the changing roles of women as breadwinners (Lawrence & Stehlik, 1996). All of these factors have multiple, domino-like impacts, resulting in serious challenges to effective human service delivery in rural and remote areas. In particular, for women with caring responsibilities, such overall disadvantage is compounded even further. Their experiences include not only a lack of adequate and appropriate support services, material hardship, and social isolation but also, in many cases, marginalisation by the communities in which they live. For example, Yvonne recalls that:

> Anyone that tried to humiliate me or put me down certainly never ever attempted it the second time around. I became very used to it. I expected it and I knew how to defend myself against it … (Bowden, 1995, p. 220).

Our landscape, its geographic size and population spread, has historically demanded unique responses to the tyranny of distance, as we discuss further in Chapter 2. For example, in the past decade, a national adaptive response has resulted in a marked increase in the number of professionals who now fly-in/fly-out (FiFo) of their workplaces. Commencing initially as a response to the mining boom of the early 2000s, and primarily then focused on engineers and geologists, it is now becoming more institutionalised in other professional settings (traditionally seen as the caring professions), including health services, social work services, and education services. The costs associated with this approach remain prohibitive. In addition, most recently, telecommunications have begun to include a trend towards 'telehealth' as we discuss further in Chapter 5.

To summarise, the issue of regions in Australia has a long history, from the earliest years of European settlement. The constant push/pull between the urban and the regional (and rural) remains of interest not only academically but also politically. This issue is one that challenges concepts of place, memory, and diversity, as we discuss further in other chapters. It is also a truism that 'rural' and 'remote' have more political 'value' during the lead-up to elections than at any other time. Those who live beyond the urban coastal settlements know this, and this explains, to some degree, the push/pull nature of their political involvement.

4 Human service delivery

The context in which human services are delivered in Australia is highly political: as both political (large scale, as in the way in which our governance operates) and political (on the ground, local, immediate).

Throughout this book, we refer to the framework that informs Australian government programs and legislation as being 'neoliberal': that is, the fundamental '... relationships between the state, market and communities ...' have shifted, and the state has been replaced by the 'market' where competition is lauded as being essential to ensure efficiency and effectiveness (Maidment & Bay, 2012, p. 226). This shift has had much impact on social work practice, including, as we discuss here, an increasing privatisation of the many programs designed to enable support for vulnerable citizens. The withdrawal of 'on the ground' government services over time has been extensive. Australia has an essentially privatised for-profit 'welfare' sector that has grown exponentially since the early 1980s, and despite many government reviews and reports, there appears to be little appetite for any fundamental change.

Social workers in rural and remote communities are not always employed by governments. As we explain in more detail in these chapters, the rural is changing, and one obvious and immediate change has been the introduction of private-for-profit business as a response to the introduction of the National Disability Insurance Scheme in 2013. This major policy changed service delivery from groups to individuals. Briefly, the individual, when assessed, gets personal funding allocated that they then spend on services and supports to meet those assessed needs. It is this market-driven, neo-liberal ideology that has changed the way in which many social workers are now employed. Under this new funding model, many large service organisations struggled to provide services, and many moved from the sector, especially in rural and remote communities. The costs of travel and the difficulties with recruitment and retention all led to large services shutting regional offices, moving to FiFo (fly-in fly-out) models, or simply leaving the area. Small businesses were established quickly to meet the need: either as managers of the services the individual was entitled to or as deliverers of those services.

Physiotherapists, occupational therapists, podiatrists, and other professionals, previously perhaps employed by government agencies or the non-government sector, opened up their own small businesses and began servicing clients. This has reached rural areas. In larger centres, entrepreneurial professionals, including social workers, have established their businesses. We discuss working in these different environments in Chapter 5.

Australia has three tiers of government: federal, state, and local. Human services can be delivered from any one of these tiers. In addition, and importantly, there are other critical players such as charities, churches, and increasingly, particularly since the late twentieth century, private for-profit organisations. Those of us who work, research, and write about this sector have used the following shorthand: NGOs. These non-government organisations, which can be either private for profit or charitable, but often very confusingly, are still funded by governments.

This complex system operates without the average 'client' either understanding or wanting to understand this complexity. It is sometimes just too much to take in. Indeed, the social work practitioner may be paid by the Federal Government through a short-term grant, through the State government as part of a program that the Federal Government funds, with some State government contributions, or by local government, which, in many rural areas, is often the only significant player. What needs to be appreciated here as you read this book is that this is a layered system, very complex, very diversified. Funding can often be short-term, meaning that practitioners are often subject to much change and different policies, with their working lives often at risk of ending. This is particularly so with changes in government. After each election, whether state or federal, programs change, money is withdrawn, and additional stress is placed on all those involved. For the average client, it also means that the 'face of the service' changes on a regular basis – we call this the 'churn' and we return to this further in Chapter 3.

The challenges associated with rural and remote service delivery can be encapsulated by one example, which continues to remain as a 'wound' on the national psyche. In 2007, the conservative Federal government, on the cusp of a national election, shocked the nation with a policy that has come to be called 'the Intervention'. As the Federal government maintains oversight on its territories – this Intervention was aimed at those First Nations communities of the Northern Territory and was in response to a strong media call and a recently received report, which argued strongly for a partnership approach to the issues outlined but which was ignored.

The strategy was in response to what was perceived as increasing levels of violence in communities and promoted as being about the safety and security of children. It was a wide-ranging approach, costing nearly A$600m, with '… restrictions on alcohol, changes to welfare payments, acquisition of parcels of land, education, employment and health initiatives, restrictions on pornography and other measures …' (Gray, 2020, p. 9). It also, to the rest of the country's surprise, included members of the Australian army to police its rollout. It was a shock to those communities to see the armed forces personnel, in full uniform, arrive and set up tent villages near their homes.

While the subsequent Federal Election in 2008 changed the government, the Intervention remained, with some alterations and some additions, in particular targeting a reform of the welfare system. We are now approaching the 20th anniversary of this policy, but it remains fundamentally at the heart of much government decision-making associated with First Nations communities. It continues to affect the lives of those living in their communities, and therefore the practice of any social workers working alongside them. In Chapter 6, we discuss just how important it is to prepare to enter any community, from the perspective of politics, but also its history, geography, and demographics.

5 Understanding rural and remote

Rural has now come to mean, 'not the city,' as if rural began in the edges of any dense urban environment. In Australia, a vast country where most of the population (over 80 per cent) live within 50 kms of its eastern and southern coastlines, 'rural' has come to be understood as 'the bush' or 'the wilderness' or in a colloquial way 'the outback' where few people live, and it continues to be vaguely understood that most of them are involved in some form of agriculture. In other large, geographically widespread countries, such as those in North America, the 'spaces' between cities were deemed 'rural,' and in Canada, the 'north' was always considered to be 'remote,' just as it has been in Australia. 'Remote' also becomes relevant when we consider some places in the United Kingdom, Ireland, or New Zealand, where geography and infrastructure access offer challenges to service delivery.

Our work has focused on a deeper understanding of rural practice through a framework of 'rurality'. UK geographer Paul Cloke
(2006) defined and refined a typology of 'rurality' over 30 years
ago. He identified several components: population density and
population change; household structure; mobility; occupational structure; and distance from nearest urban centres. Nicole
Rousseau (1995) undertook to answer the question: What is
rurality? in the context of the delivery of health services in Great
Britain. She found that few researchers, if any, attempted a form
of definition, and when they did, the variety of definitions not
only tended to focus on deprivation but also made comparisons
difficult. She came to the conclusion that it was '… difficult to
choose any one feature which captures the essence of rurality
…' (p. 3).

In particular, and importantly for this book, Cloke reminds us that
… 'the concept of rurality lives on in the popular imagination
and everyday practices of the contemporary world …' (p. 18). In
other words, we can think of 'rural' (and remote) as both fixed,
real places as well as one in our (and others') imagination. Cloke's
typology and others like it have led to governments devising
methods to gather data, such as census data, to assist them in
delivering services.

Importantly here in this introduction, we want to stress just
how rurality can help us understand 'the rural' as being something more than just geographic, occupation, and population-
based. It is highly political and highly politicised. Historically, in
Australia, as in other countries, politics have been, and continue
to be, shaped by urban/rural complexities. We will be stressing
throughout this book, and on a regular basis, that a social work

practitioner works within a highly political setting – whether they are located in a city, a suburb, or in a remote community. Understanding how important this context is a critical step in enabling their ethical practice.

To better understand the concept of rurality as it applies to present-day Australia, we also need to understand the language associated with 'rural', 'regional', and 'remote'. These terms emerged strongly in human service practice and policy at the same time as Australia experienced the most severe drought since European settlement (1788). This event, which came to be called the Millennium Drought, spanned nearly two decades from the early 1990s until around 2010. The power of this lack of rainfall across most of settled Australia, which culminated in shocking the urban population by a lack of water for the cities, created an environment where, politically, rural Australia began to call for redefinitions. Nationally, we began to hear more about how important place was to those who were living through these hard times. By place here, we mean something much more than geography, as we describe in further detail in Chapter 4.

For this overview, the outcome of this challenge of drought was that 'rural' became diminished in importance even further, and 'regional' became the growth focus. Regional gained strength and purpose as it was not rural. Regional Australia was defined to the 'east' of the Great Dividing Range, the large escarpment that runs the length of the country from Far North Queensland to Victoria and acts as an important watershed for the cities. It is also near the coast and therefore holds most of the population, as we have explained. Regional Australia could be supported by governments and was encouraged to grow economically beyond just primary production, largely through tourism and resource extraction, because it was near the coast and therefore more desirable.

This change also meant that rural Australia was less well able to compete or to be supported. It became an issue that if there was no water, what was the point of any investment in infrastructure? Historically, small communities in rural environments have always been 'hollowed out' as population decline meant fewer residents. However, this major change in climate accelerated the process, and one response we heard was that 'tiny towns must die.' This was where the strength and resilience of place identity became a powerful determinant, as the backlash to these urban-centric policies gathered momentum. One community, Barcaldine in far western Queensland (over 1,000 kms or an 11-hour drive from Brisbane), can represent many. Its population declined by 15 per cent between 2003 and 2023 (from around 1,770 to 1,540). These are small numbers, which makes the decline even sharper for those who live there. These small communities are vulnerable to rumours about mines reopening, which brings some hope for the locals who often make decisions accordingly, such as occurred in the small town of Alpha nearby to Barcaldine in 2006. These rumours proved to be false, and the community was then left disappointed and often with an economic shortfall (Nakamura & Walsh (2024) Once bustling country towns losing people as industries, youth move away (https://apple.new/AfN u3TAL1Rw2bl-HylsuH8g Accessed: 13th November, 2024.)

Briefly, it is important to underline here how the impact of the COVID-19 pandemic changed the relationships between urban and rural Australia. As lockdowns proceeded, Australians decided to explore their own country instead of travelling overseas. They bought caravans and motor homes and began travelling the 'outback' roads. Free camping was available, often on farm properties that were also finding life hard going, and were glad of the visitors. This new form of 'mobile tourism' began to change the way in which small communities welcomed the visitors. For example, Winton, in western Queensland, made the most of this influx by embracing the tourism potential of many local assets. Rare dinosaur fossils had been discovered some years ago on a local cattle property. The local grazier owner of the station saw the potential this had for tourism and, in partnership with the state's natural museum, the local council, and the whole community, has developed a world-class dinosaur centre attracting thousands of visitors each year. This initiative stimulated other ventures in the town, including a local gallery, an annual film festival, and a dark sky sanctuary. These attractions employ local people and backpackers as well as other visitors, and are now an integral part of the local economy.

In this section, we have explained some terms that will continue to appear in subsequent chapters such as rural, rurality, stereotyping, and others. We have briefly outlined how Australia's history has shaped modern-day understanding of what it means to be rural, and the considered attributes associated with stereotypes that conjure up images, both positive and negative, of those who live beyond our cities. We have also very briefly touched on just how this impacts our social work practice.

The next section describes the evidence we use throughout the book drawn from our collaborations. We note that all those who contributed and whose voices we call on here have been given pseudonyms to maintain their confidentiality.

6 Gathering the evidence

Our collaboration began in the early 1990s when one of us (Daniela) moved from Western Australia to central Queensland to join the local regional university there. At that time, Lesley was living and working in a university in Brisbane but had been born and grown up in Rockhampton, the city that Daniela now lived in.

We commenced our collaboration over a small project funded by a non-government agency focused on a new approach to the delivery of social services in a regional city north of Brisbane. Lesley was a social worker who had recently become a university educator. Daniela was trained as a social scientist. At that time, both of us had also just started our postgraduate studies towards a degree of Doctor of Philosophy in different Australian universities. We quickly recognised the value of our collaboration. It gave us a strength of purpose, a way of extending our research interests, and, importantly, it was fundamentally underpinned by our shared values and trusted friendship. (We wrote about this and how we go about our collaborations in a journal article published as Stehlik & Chenoweth (2005).

We celebrated our first published collaboration called:'Interpreting Human Service Policy in Regional and Rural Queensland: The Practitioners' Perspective' in 1999. So, this book takes us both full circle back to that very first publication, and we are pleased that we have been given this opportunity to revisit our experiences over the past 25 years, bring them up to date, and share them here with you, our reader.

This early experience gave us the confidence to continue to apply for grants and, later, to expand our research beyond Queensland to Western Australia and the Northern Territory, as well as to invite colleagues and postgraduate students to join us. In this book, we touch on findings from research we conducted with a grant from the Australian Research Council (DP0988473 Managing tensions in professional statutory practice: living and working in rural and remote communities), a study of some 800 professionals (nursing, social work, education, and police) working in rural and remote Queensland, including professionals working with Aboriginal and Torres Strait Islander communities in Far North Queensland (FNQ). This research resulted in our deeper appreciation of how practice impacts the roles of professionals in small communities, where they may be located for several consecutive days but do not live permanently. Some examples include the juggling of relationships (personal and professional), the boundaries of professionalism, maintaining confidentiality, and role-specific tensions. We became particularly interested in the motivations that underpin the decision to work rurally and to continue to do so, or, alternatively, to leave. We now argue that such decisions have a degree of activism associated with them; whereby the professional understands that they are both an advocate for place specifically and 'the rural' more broadly. In other words, the motivation to work outside urban settings comes with an appreciation of this fact. We concluded that the recruitment and retention of professionals were influenced by place as much as by the actual physical nature of the job itself and its workload.

This large, national study confirmed and extended our previous projects, which, over the years, also came to include several major tasks for state governments, evaluating programs that placed new practitioners in smaller settings with a focus on service delivery to vulnerable people. Two projects, in particular, stand out for the lessons we learned about rural and remote practice and which evidence we draw on here, including some words from the practitioners themselves. These were funded by the Queensland and New South Wales governments and were to evaluate, over a reasonably long period of time, the introduction of what were called Local Area Coordinators (LAC) into small rural and remote communities that had previously had little or no service delivery to vulnerable residents, in these cases, people with a disability.

The LAC program was designed very strongly on bounded places, with a view that the practitioners would gain a really deep knowledge of the strengths, resources, and challenges of that place and those communities as a way of strengthening their practice. These projects were a powerful reminder to us both of the power of place and place identity. Our research highlighted just how the impact of a program designed within an urban setting, despite what may be best intentions, tends to miss the nuances of living and working in rural environments. This became our constant message that we shared through our many publications, presentations, and through our teaching programs with student practitioners. We will return to this further in the next chapter, in which we also explain how this bias towards the urban nature of service delivery policy and programs has to be continually reshaped, redefined, and often challenged when being delivered rurally by the individual professional.

There are many lessons that have emerged from our collaboration over the past two and a half decades, many of which we have also been able to share with government agencies, the non-government sector, and private service delivery organisations. We both consider ourselves to be advocates for social service practice in rural and remote settings, and we hope that this book and the comprehensive evidence we provide here continue to give you, the reader, the strengths necessary to continue that advocacy.

The final section of this introduction provides a brief outline of how we have structured the book itself. Each chapter 'stands alone' and can be read in that way, or the reader can begin at the beginning and work their way through to the end. We provide you with some reflective questions at the end of each chapter as these may give you the interest to go deeper into the subject matter, perhaps through the reference list at the end of the book.

7 Book structure

The book is divided into six chapters. Following this introduction, Chapter 2 on rural and remote practice offers a brief history and key features of social policy and social services in rural and remote places. We also describe how the differences between urban and rural practice can be explained, and what the challenges and opportunities are for social workers working in these settings.

Chapter 3 is titled the paradox of 'community' and we consider community here as both experience and construction. We particularly focus on the way in which government policies, created in urban settings, shape and dominate the ways in which the practitioner can and cannot practice.

We have titled Chapter 4 the power of 'place' where we analyze the complex relationships between understandings of place and our ability to provide ethical practice. We touch on here how the value and critical importance place has for First Nations communities and how the practitioner can both enhance and support this value.

Chapter 5 draws all these threads together in what we have called Community-focussed resource-based practice. We describe the strengths and challenges of this approach: the dilemmas we can face as practitioners, how to avoid ethical conundrums while at the same time strengthening our advocacy for our clients. We have a conclusions chapter at 6, where we highlight just how important advocacy for place is as a fundamental platform for practice. We offer a timeline to the new practitioner. Finally, we will look to the future possibilities for rural social work and the role of practitioners in shaping and advocating for rural communities.

In our next chapter, we consider the nature of social work practice in rural and remote communities and highlight the differences between rural social work and other fields of practice.

Reflections from your experience

What images are conjured up in your mind when you think about 'rural'?

How is 'the rural' described currently? What are the words specifically and what do they imply?

What are some common stereotypes associated with living rurally?

2
Rural and remote practice

Learning objectives

- Describe aspects of the history and key features of social policy and social work in rural and remote places.
- Outline the key differences between urban-based and rural and remote practice – approaches and methods.
- Articulate the challenges of recruitment and retention for social workers working in these settings.

1 Introduction

In our previous chapter, we outlined the purpose of the book and of our collaboration in rural, regional, and remote Australian communities with the social workers and other practitioners who live and work in them. We also provided a brief historical context when considering rural Australia and the services available.

In this chapter, we delve deeper into the nature of social work practice in rural and remote communities. We begin by offering a brief history of the services and contexts that constitute rural areas and rural social work. We will then explore the differences between rural social work and other contexts and fields of practice. The main body of this chapter explores the features of rural social work: who are these practitioners? What are their challenges and opportunities? It concludes with a detailed discussion of the aspects of recruitment and retention of social work practitioners in rural and remote communities as determined by a large national study we led and other research we have completed.

2 A brief history of rural services and rural social work

As we begin to consider the history of social work in Australia, we must take into account that social work in this country is very much a product of the country's colonisation. This remains a foundation for current practices. The many settlements that later formed our cities soon faced entrenched social problems, and from the early nineteenth century, charitable organisations were established to provide support to the destitute, to pregnant women, and to children. These charities were supported by the colonial governors (prior to Federation) and represented the earliest responses to many needs. In time, hospitals and asylums, following the British model, were established; for example, the Benevolent Society established in 1813 is still operating today (Benevolent Society https://www.benevolent.org.au Accessed: 23rd November 2024).

As the population of Australia grew, there was an increase in migration beyond the coastlines into the inland, as the search for agricultural land and mining opportunities drew settlers. Few services followed them, and the long distances from cities and isolation from the main centres created challenges that were difficult to address. It was not until the mid-twentieth century that we encounter any real social work responses in rural communities. In the decades post-WW2, the framework of a welfare state was established, which in turn created offices in some of the larger centres that, by the mid-1970s, were providing health services, child protection services, social security, and the Commonwealth Employment Service.

3 Social work education

The earliest formal training of social workers was through separate training bodies for social workers and almoners linked to organisations such as the Red Cross and hospitals. The serious efforts to establish university-based social work education in Australia began before WW2. Predictably, the social work degrees were offered in the major cities and at Australia's oldest universities in Sydney, Melbourne, and Adelaide. By 1942 all three universities were offering social studies/social work degrees (Lawrence, 1965). Other states followed, initially offering three year degrees. The University of Queensland began teaching social work in a Bachelor of Social Studies in 1954, which was upgraded to a four-year degree in the 1960s. These courses included significant practicums across different agencies, mostly in the city. Here, Lesley recalls her own experiences:

> As a girl growing up in a country town and attending an all-girls school, the options for girls post-school were limited. My friends became secretaries, shop assistants, trained as nurses in hospitals or went away to teaching college. In my class of some 45 girls, only six of us went on to university. I received an offer and a scholarship to attend the only university in the state some 700km away.

The idea of social work as a career had never occurred to me. I had never met a social worker. Certainly, there weren't any working where I lived. I had a vague idea that they 'helped people'. When I had to make the decision to nominate what degree I would study, I had no clue. Of my friends three chose Arts and two the Sciences. In a valiant attempt to be different, I wrote Bachelor of Social Studies on my application and I moved away from the country town to the largest city in the state. On reflection this was a bold move for someone barely 17 and who had lived with her family in the same town until then. Being 'away' was hard. I missed home and family.

The course was oriented to psychology, sociology, economics and heavy on theory. It was a welcome relief to have my first practicum experience in a large city hospital. The social work subjects were strongly focussed on method – direct case work, group work, counselling and later community work. Over the four years, I completed four 'pracs' all located in city environments, including one in a government social security department in another state capital. It was here I had my first brief entrée into rural social work. As part of the office 'outreach' I made several home visits to struggling families in remote farming areas. The inequities were immediately apparent - poverty, poor living conditions, sickness and few services. (Lesley).

It was not until the late 1960s and 1970s that practicing social workers were employed in areas outside of the capital cities. This began in government agencies in larger population centres, such as the practicums described above, then expanded through outreach (which meant travelling) to provide some level of service to people living in rural, and later, more remote, communities. There were funds provided to enable social workers to pay visits to other nearby towns, perhaps weekly or monthly. These services were few and far between, as were the numbers of social workers who were able and willing to undertake this form of practice. Lesley continues:

> My first experience of rural practice could best be described as an accident. Needing a job in a provincial town where social work was still relatively unknown, an opportunity to work in a newly created community health centre was very appealing. I always enjoyed a new challenge outside the square, it was a government position so secure in tenure and, as a relatively new graduate, the prospects for furthering my knowledge and skills were good. In the initial few months, I was on a fast track acquiring knowledge about health services, health social work and working in a team with nurses, psychologists and occupational therapists and physiotherapists. Very quickly we were faced with numerous and diverse community needs and demands from outlying areas beyond the town for services. Within six months we were driving to other small towns and villages, doing outreach visits and trying to provide what help we could to people who had had virtually no community-based services. At the same time, very few of us had had experience of working with community. Armed with a fairly generic but thorough, social work training, I was quickly drawing on my previous (brief) experience as a caseworker in

a general welfare setting and going back to my notes on group work. (Lesley)

4 What is rural social work?

As social work practice in rural communities spans the spectrum of social work fields, methods, and interventions, it is more helpful, therefore, to think of rural social work as 'not one thing' but rather as a descriptive term that relates to social work's location and context in regional, rural, and remote areas (Pugh & Cheers, 2010).

Rural social workers support people in accessing health services, deliver social care to people with disabilities or older adults, respond to families experiencing financial difficulty, and assist women and children escaping domestic violence. Increasingly, rural practitioners are also becoming early responders to natural disasters such as bushfires or floods (Stehlik, 2013). For the most part, one would find these activities across all other social work fields and contexts, in inner cities, in large organisations and government agencies, in city suburbs, and in sprawling outer suburban housing developments. However, as we discuss in this book, there are differences for rural social work, particularly factors of geography, isolation, and long distances. In addition, and importantly, the politics of rural that we discuss in detail in the next chapter create a social policy milieu that establishes policies and initiatives without 'rural' in mind and for communities that are poorly resourced in terms of adjunct support services.

A number of approaches to rural social work have emerged over decades. It is interesting to note that there were considerable international publications on rural social work in the 1990s and early 2000s, though these were mostly country-specific. The literature has largely been silent on the topic now for more than a decade, although the practice remains well and truly alive. We note that rural social work has gained some attention most recently, especially in the United Kingdom (Turbett & Pyne, 2024), the United States (Daley, 2021), and Australia (Maidment & Bay, 2021).

We now consider two main approaches to rural social work: generalist and community-embedded practice and how they are applied.

4.1 Generalist practice

The notion of the rural social worker as a generalist has been a strong and enduring concept. Generalist social work considers problems on all levels – the micro, meso, and macro – and uses a wide range of intervention methods to work with families, groups, individuals, and communities. In the course of their work, generalist social workers engage, assess, and offer counseling; they broker services, advocate for better policies and programs; and they organise, build capacity alongside, and with communities (Gasker, 2023).

Generalists do not take one specific approach but rather draw across a whole spectrum of approaches. Practicing as a generalist means entering any situation ready to assess every angle, to tackle problems for an individual, a particular group, or by advocating for a whole community.

Many of the practitioners we have met during our research activities talk about having to rapidly build a range of skills and knowledge in response to the presenting problems. This means having to quickly learn how to navigate complex cases. For example, Cheryl worked in rural communities in Australia for several decades. Here, she reflects on how her early training in Sydney gave her the capacity to be holistic in her approach in different rural settings.

> In my training you learnt casework, you learnt group work, you learned about community work. You learned about all sorts of methods and interventions. … You'd have an unmarried mother in your caseload and then another, or a young new mum and soon you'd have a few more and you would set up a mothers' group … (Cheryl).

When asked about the rapid learning curve needed to navigate such complex problems, she adds, 'You just gotta sit down and work things out!'

When we talk about being a generalist, this should not be taken to mean lacking depth for specialisation. The generalist social worker, such as Cheryl, is informed by an extensive knowledge base and a range of skills and interventions. Her practice is founded on core values of social justice and empowerment and guided by a code of ethics. The specialisation here is the capacity to assess the situation and respond to the range of needs and issues for people in rural communities.

4.2 Community embedded practice

Community-embedded practice draws upon ideas from community development, community planning, and community work interventions. Let's consider the standpoint of the social worker finding themselves in a rural community facing a number of challenges. It soon becomes apparent that there are no obvious public or private services available, and they will need to search for solutions locally. This inevitably means working across traditional service boundaries within and with the broader community.

These approaches are well documented in the literature across several countries; for example, Emilia Martinez-Brawley (1990; 2000) with small communities in the United States in the 1990s and early 2000s and later in Scotland was a powerful advocate of these approaches. In Australia, Brian Cheers (1998) and others' research and writings drew on community work knowledge and methods to further develop this approach for rural social work. In the UK, Richard Pugh (2003), and more recently, Turbett & Pye (2024) similarly devote much attention to working in community-embedded ways.

As we consider the late twentieth century, we can observe, with the advent of social policies and programs based on neo-liberalist ideologies, how social services become more specialised and narrower in focus as a strategy to gain more apparent efficiency. Generalist and community-based approaches became displaced by highly specialised services targeted at specific individual problems with funding attached to the individual. However, rural communities were often unable to provide such services in small populations with little infrastructure and also struggled to recruit suitable professional staff even if such services were available.

Practice that is grounded in community development, community planning, and community social work is therefore central to rural social work (Lynch, Forde & Lathouras, 2020). While community work is undertaken in other practice contexts, the embedded aspects of rural social work come from the fundamental reality of the practitioner working in and living in the community. That is, they are embedded in the places, social relationships, and interconnections of home, family, friends, and workplace. We discuss the importance of place further in Chapter 4. Here we stress that community practice can be understood as foundational to a strong commitment to partnership and community participation based on the following principles:

- the routine involvement of local people in planning, developing and organising local services;
- the promotion of democracy and empowerment in decision-making and recognition of the strength and assets of local people and organisations;
- the advancement of common interests over private, organisational or professional interests; and,
- the promotion of social and economic justice (Pugh & Cheers, 2010, p. 153).

Additionally, most approaches recognise that rural social services, and the lives of the people who use them, as well as the lives of the staff who work in them, are interlinked with other sectors such as the local economy, industry, health, and education. These approaches recognise that changes in one sector are likely to impact others. Perhaps the most significant impacts occur when crucial local businesses close in rural communities, as the following constructed example illustrates:

> Many small rural towns in Australia rely on one major employer. In Morrisville this was the abattoir servicing the surrounding grazing industry. After several years of

serious drought, the abattoir declined in output and finally was closed by the urban-based company that owned it. More than 70 people lost their jobs. Within a few months, several people and families moved away seeking employment and other income. With the decrease in population, the bank, shops and even the pharmacy reduced its hours along with the visiting general practitioner. This loss of population meant that the local primary school was no longer viable, and it was closed. Students were then bussed to the next nearest centre.

Over the ensuing years, this creates a domino effect whereby decreasing population leads to reduced services, which in turn can lead to further population decline.

5 Who are rural social workers?

We now explore the who of rural social work in Australia. Who are these workers and how did they get here? In Australia, the recruiting and supporting of practitioners in rural areas has proven to be difficult and challenging for most non-urban parts of the country, with many positions remaining unfilled for long periods of time. Problems of distance and lack of community services continue to pose a major challenge to recruitment, retention, and practice. In Australia, a larger proportion of new graduates are often appointed to rural positions, with the result that many do not remain in these positions for long, thereby creating a practice climate of instability. Agencies are chronically understaffed and may spend considerable time and resources recruiting and training new workers only to see them leave a short time later – often less than a year. After a couple of these cycles, recruitment becomes a kind of 'churn'. The exiting practitioner may not see the impact of their contribution – you can't see the fruits of your labour. In our experience, some rural agencies have positions that remain unfilled for years or have people in the role intermittently. We touch further on the concept of 'churn' in Chapter 3.

In our work, we have encountered a wide range of practitioner stories and experiences. Some new appointees arrive, quickly become disillusioned, and soon leave. Others have grown up in rural communities and are committed to them, while some come for several years for opportunities for lifestyle change or are seeking career advancement. This next section offers a typology of practitioners that we developed over time, particularly when undertaking our nation-wide study for the Australian Research Council over three years.

5.1 The rurally committed

This group consists of those practitioners who have worked in the rural and remote context for most of their working life, either in the same rural community or in a variety of rural settings. They may have been born in the area or moved from elsewhere, but they have certainly lived and worked in the community for many years. These workers tend to have strong links with the community, not just through their professional role. 'Committeds' typically have other key roles within local organisations and networks and demonstrate resilience, practicality, confidence, skills in problem-solving, as well as a capacity to not personalise the job. They are also mature, respect others, and have a strong desire or passion to work in the area. They are not easily intimidated and tend to be extroverted, with good communication and negotiation skills. For example, Annie and Lyn from a coastal town put it this way:

> ... you do have to have a tough, tough personality. You do. (Annie)
>
> Outgoing people. People with strong extroverted personalities are generally the people who will stay; who will be able to hack it out. (Lyn)

This group also tends to act as gatekeepers of information about local history and practice precedents (i.e. how things are done). However, due to their long-term experience, they may also have set ideas about the way to do things. We noted a tendency of some of these workers to disregard new ideas or be overtly sceptical about new practice approaches that could be required by central decision-makers.

> Look when you've been here for this long, you know what has worked and what hasn't. We tried that five years ago and it didn't work. So why go there again? (Sandra).

Those who stay represent a valuable resource in rural agencies. They like rural work and are strong, experienced workers who contribute over the long term. Working with them, like Sandra, can be daunting for new recruits. Due to their experience and confidence, they can inhibit new workers and even inadvertently contribute to their leaving rural positions. As Deb, who worked for a non-government agency in a regional centre, put it:

> People with life experiences generally hold it out better. People who have got the experience of being able to

look to the community for part of what they need for social support, personal support might be a useful way of going about that. (Deb).

Our research concluded that this group's contribution as mentors, supervisors, and practice leaders can be fostered through offering professional development and leadership opportunities. These need to be flexibly delivered so that knowledge and capacity building can be developed on-site rather than in the capital city or major centre, far from the local office.

5.2 Leavers

In following up the reasons why social workers left some rural communities, we found, to our surprise, that many were uninformed or misinformed about the nature of rural locations and what to expect even prior to taking up their positions. As Rosemary, when thinking about a new recruit, remembered that:

She arrived and made the comment that ' this is a long way from the beach' – like it is a 6 hour drive to the coast! (Rosemary).

In these situations, it is both the rural location and a realisation that living in rural communities is personally untenable that can prompt the person to leave. In other situations, we noted that experiencing the nature of the work, i.e. child protection, which can be personally challenging, was also a contributing factor. This again links to the practitioner's orientation and induction. Several of those practitioners who participated in our study and had been employed for only one or two months were actively looking for other positions and wanted to leave as soon as possible. This aspect can be as confronting in a larger centre as in a smaller, remote setting, as Bill suggests:

> … if you're a personality type that is offended easily and frightened easily you aren't going to last [here] … (Bill).

'Leavers' are not attracted to the rural/outdoors lifestyle and prefer urban communities. They do not usually have strong links with the community in which they are located and are not interested in developing networks as a way of coping. Leavers can show characteristics such as being easily intimidated, and are perhaps, to some degree, introverted, and their social contacts and networks tend to be focused outside the community.

While personal attributes tend to characterise 'Leavers', the aspects of the community can also contribute to their departure from positions. For example, some communities are not particularly welcoming to outsiders, making it difficult for them to continue working in them. Beth, from a small, reasonably remote community, described it as:

> .. very cliquey … and if you're an outsider, they don't accept outsiders very well. [W]hen I was working out there I found them very non-accepting of anything outside of what their expected norm was, and so I found that really difficult. (Beth).

'Leavers' can be both disruptive and costly for organisations in rural and remote locations. Recruitment and induction processes involve significant fiscal and human resources such that having a person start on day one already represents a considerable investment, both financial and emotional. The key strategy for rural agencies is therefore to avoid the recruitment of potential

'Leavers' through such measures as adopting better screening of potential applicants in the recruitment stage, ensuring that induction orientation makes no assumptions about rural/remote practice, and also ensuring that a mentor or buddy system is in place at the new location.

Social work and human service educators have a role to play here. Our study of new graduates showed that approximately half had very little or no understanding of rural life or rural practice and that degree programs largely did not prepare students well for rural work (McAuliffe, Chenoweth & Stehlik, 2007). Potential 'Leavers' could perhaps be assisted to self-identify during their university training if better preparation through experiential learning programs in a rural context was provided, enabling them to gain a better appreciation of the issues involved with working and living in rural and remote communities before applying for such positions. We will return to the theme of how to enter a new place in Chapter 6.

Finally, a further impediment to recruitment in the long term is the potential of former 'Leavers' to deter future applicants through hearsay and, more recently, the power and reach of social media.

5.3 Sea-changers/tree-changers

An emerging group of recruits to regional and rural positions are those we have called 'sea-changers' or 'tree-changers'. The term 'sea-changer' is used in a metaphorical sense to describe people who are looking for a fundamental lifestyle change (Murphy, 2002). In Australia, this group is usually associated with moves from urban centres to smaller coastal centres, though increasingly it also includes those seeking non-coastal locations within commuting distance of larger cities (i.e., 'tree-changers'). While this group can include retirees looking for a lifestyle change based on better recreational options and cheaper living costs, it also includes those prior to retirement who may be seeking ongoing employment for at least a few years while making changes to their lifestyle in a new setting. Sharon describes her own decision-making:

> Oh look, I made a pretty clear and conscious decision to leave my lifestyle and career of 16 years in [other state] to move up here. So I've probably got my short to medium term goals ... short to medium would be three to five years. (Sharon).

In our interviews and focus groups, we encountered several practitioners in this situation and believe that this group holds significant under-realised potential for future recruitment. 'Sea/tree-changers' may have strong capabilities with leadership potential and often bring relevant human service and public service experience with them. 'Sea/tree-changers' usually have strong motivation to establish ties within the local community as they have deliberately chosen this place to make their home. They may also be older workers, planning for retirement, so regard employment as a way into social networks in local communities. Sharon goes on to explain:

> ... it was nice to go into the local supermarket [or the] the local newsagent and know the person behind the counter. You might actually play golf with them on Saturday and things. (Sharon)

Due to their lifestyle choices, this group may not be attracted to all sites, so may be a resource for particular locations only. Nevertheless, reinforcing their decision to move to a rural or

remote community should impact the retention of these workers. Lucy and Jodie reflect on this:

> I relocated here in 2004 I think; 2003 maybe. After work-
> ing for 12 years in a southern state. Yeah and saw the
> light and moved north to the warm weather. (Lucy).
>
> So I suppose some people might argue that being
> anonymous is a good thing where others might say
> they like having an identity; being a part of the com-
> munity. (Jodie).

5.4 'Grow your own'

In all locations, participants identified employees who were local
people who may have entered human service work as front-line
unskilled workers on a part-time or casual basis but who then
demonstrated aptitude and ability for long-term employment
(Tilbury, Aitchison, Chenoweth, McAuliffe, Stehlik, & Osmond
(2014). A number of these locals then embarked on university
degrees in distance mode and were studying or had already completed their formal qualifications on the job. This group is more
likely to stay in positions, given the importance of family and community networks in retention. Judy, working in a regional centre for
a non-government agency, reflects on this group and its potential:

> So to recruit people [to] organisations like ours, I would
> like to see [some] offering support to locals to get their
> qualification because there's just not [the] people [avail-
> able] … and we've got to support [the locals] through
> that process. (Judy)

Local people with potential include Indigenous workers who
bring valuable local knowledge, links to the community, and

hands-on capability. Many of these people are strongly committed to place and therefore pose fewer retention issues. However, they may not have access to university programs or other tertiary training and are often limited in their career paths. In addition, the agency or organisation that employs them may not recognise their potential and thus not mentor or support them.

The presence of 'Locals with potential' in all sites of our study highlighted the need to determine innovative learning pathways whereby potential recruits could enter human service work at the local level and acquire necessary qualifications as they gained experience on the job. This would require flexibly delivered courses, with recognition of on-site learning and prior experience for admission, as well as support from local communities for educating and training these workers. For example, there may be scope for an apprenticeship-style model for these workers. A key issue that arose for locals was that of juggling allegiances and negotiating the dual relationships that arise from working and living in a rural setting (Jervis-Tracey, Chenoweth, McAuliffe, Stehlik & O'Connor (2012) This would need to be identified as part of any training.

5.5 Mid-term career movers

Another group that emerged from our research are what we have termed 'mid-term Career Movers'. This group consisted of fairly experienced practitioners from a capital city or larger regional centres who took up positions in rural offices to gain broader experience, to act in leadership positions, and then return to central office at a higher level. Others in this group saw a rural position in, for example, child protection, as a way to change career direction from a different field such as education or policing. The decision to take up a rural position was, for some, a deliberate strategy to further their career aspirations. For others, it was less planned, but a time in the country certainly facilitated a faster rise on the career ladder. They were also individuals for whom such moves made career sense. As Daryl in a small centre observed:

> Somebody who stays here for two years suddenly gets bumped up to PO4, PO5 [elsewhere] as a Team Leader. (Daryl).

Social workers with career aspirations will contribute at a high level and will be conscious of performing well in any new role. However, they will also move on if they are unhappy with a work situation/environment. Recruitment efforts could be directed at practitioners thinking or wishing to change careers but who are prepared to move to a rural community. Many of these practitioners would bring considerable professional expertise, knowledge, and skills to rural agencies though would not necessarily have the local knowledge or networks. Support to form links with the local community would also be a priority to ensure their retention. This group is also more likely to have children and therefore be seeking good access to schools, sporting, and health services. Daryl makes this further point:

> Okay. … there's no reason why you can't say to people come to [these communities]. We have good schools. Bring your children aged 5 to 15. Bring your families. This is a nice quiet [place]; this [has] a nice rural ethos. It's a safe community. (Daryl)

Another issue for a mid-term 'Career Mover' is the length of time they might stay in one position. Many community members highlight the turnover in rural offices and it may be necessary to reconsider what is an adequate length of time to make a contribution. To stay for a two-year period may be attractive to many mid-term 'Career Movers' but this may be viewed as too short a timeframe for those who are already established in the office. We also noted that several participants identified a need for rural practitioners to have opportunities for mid-term career advancement in city offices or for policy or project work to be undertaken in rural offices by rural practitioners.

5.6 New graduates

Historically, the 'New Graduate' is seen as the most likely recruit to rural positions. There were two groups of new graduates identified in our study: first, the new graduates from the city who take up rural posts and second, new graduates from rural areas who return from their university studies in a large centre to their hometown or another rural community. Regardless of their backgrounds, two important challenges face this new recruit: the need to juggle multiple roles and relationships and to get connected with the local community.

Graduates' need in-service opportunities immediately. Due to generational differences, this group of workers also generally needs to be nurtured and can be easily intimidated, especially by those long-term locals who can act as powerful gatekeepers. Diane, who works in child protection, put it this way:

> The young graduates that come here who've had very fulfilling childhoods and very safe environments that they've grown up in and they've been nurtured and [had] all the things our children should receive; then they come here and see the horrendous things that happen

to some children by their own parents and have to deal with aggression that they've never ever seen; sometimes that's a very daunting thing for people. And a lot of the time people will leave because of that. (Diane).

However, our research found that given the right conditions and support, this group has the capacity to commit to rural work. For those from outside the community, support is needed to assist them in developing relationships and links to the community. This is well understood by many rural practitioners who have devised creative strategies to foster relationships between new graduates and local people. Sarah and Kylie recall that:

Well, of course you know we all get in the office and then we start matchmaking. [Laughter] You know it's true. (Sarah)
We had a young graduate and I said like 'has she got a boyfriend?' I said we could marry her off to someone that lives in [other town]. (Kylie)

For local recent graduates, the issues associated with juggling allegiances in rural and remote communities need to be addressed through educational preparation, professional development, and the establishment of mentoring/buddy systems, as well as having access to professional supervision. Rural placements in the course of university study can provide an entrée into this work, as we discuss in Chapter 6.

6 Challenges, opportunities and being 'on the ground'

There are many experiences associated with rural practice. Certainly, there are challenges of isolation, fewer services, higher workloads, and more problems stemming from general socio-economic dis-advantage. Researching social workers in rural Australia, Kreig Mayer (2001) highlighted these challenges in the context of little or no sec-ondary referral points or after-hours services and vast distances. As we have already witnessed in some practitioner accounts, these chal-lenges require other characteristics such as flexibility, creativity, tak-ing on tasks outside the actual job description, and being persistent. However, these very attributes also present positive opportunities. Rural practitioners report increased skills in community organising,, responding to natural disasters, advocacy, and having the opportu-nity to embrace new approaches in outreach such as fly-in fly-out (FiFO) and online platforms, as detailed further in Chapter 5.

Many features of all social work practice – applying a broad knowledge base, resolving ethical dilemmas, working with technology, navigating a range of systems – all routinely apply in rural settings. We suggest, however, that these are amplified or intensified in rural practice in ways that are both challenging and rewarding. It perhaps requires more critical reflection and problem-solving, but it also brings opportunities for creative and innovative practice. We now turn to two key characteristics of social work and explore how they play out in rural settings.

6.1 Dual relationships

A recurring aspect of social work in rural practice is that of dual relationships that require negotiating to enable a delicate bal-ance. The ethical dilemmas of dual relationships in rural social work practice have been well documented (Martinez-Brawley, 2000; Chenoweth & Stehlik, 2001; Chenoweth, 2004; Pugh, 2007). These accounts outline not only the inevitability of dual relationships in rural and remote settings but also acknowledge the strain on professionals trying to work within organisational parameters, legislative frameworks, and ethical codes of conduct.

In smaller communities, one will often be both a community member and a professional employed to serve the community, having to juggle these relationships. You might have kids at the same school, or you might be a volunteer with the rural fire services alongside someone who is also a client at your agency. Dual relationships create several challenges and ethical dilemmas. For example, core social work values of confidentiality and anonymity can be tricky to navigate, as Jenni explains:

> Look if someone comes and parks their car outside our agency, people will ask – why was D at your place yesterday? Everything OK? And you have to be very clear – you cannot discuss personal matters. Once you make that clear a few times, I find that people usually respect that privacy. (Jenni).

In small communities, the options for social relationships outside of work can be reduced, and navigating this can be even more difficult if you work in a statutory agency such as child protection. One of our respondents described it as 'living in a fishbowl where anything you do can be interpreted as a reflection on your professional practice'. We encountered practitioners in statutory agencies who chose to socialise with other workers in neighbouring towns where they were less known (Chenoweth & McAuliffe, 2021). Jenni explains:

> You can be judged if you go to the pub for example or are seen having a few drinks. So we pretty much work

> in A and socialise in B (neighbouring town over 50 km away) at the weekends. (Jenni).

Other practitioners welcomed the small-town vibe of being known in the community and feeling they were connected to others across multiple roles. For some rural practitioners, there can be a sense of never being 'off-duty'. This is more likely in organisations experiencing staff shortages, which is a common scenario in rural and regional centres. This can then contribute to burnout and, ultimately, in some instances, lead to the social worker leaving the position.

Building relationships can be difficult as an outsider. As we discuss in more detail in Chapter 4, there is a long-standing narrative in Australia of a distinct divide between the city and the bush. Country people may have entrenched views of people that may mean that any new practitioner will encounter being viewed with distrust or even suspicion. It often takes time to gain trust and be accepted in communities that feel 'forgotten' or neglected by urban-centric policies and programs. Many communities have seen service professionals come and go, while others fly in and out without getting to know the 'real' community. Most of the services delivered in non-urban settings are actually managed from urban settings that are usually quite distant.

In summary, living and working in small communities poses challenges for many professionals in the execution of their daily work tasks. The juggling of multiple roles that straddle both their professional and personal worlds becomes an ongoing negotiated space of conflicting responsibilities and allegiances with increased potential for ethical dilemmas (McAuliffe, 2005).

6.2 Working in statutory environments

When the nature of the work includes a statutory requirement, that is, carrying some legal responsibilities such as mandatory reporting, policing, or the regulation of mental health patients, the frequency and intensity of these dilemmas are likely to be increased. Some examples include highly publicised events such as the Intervention in the Northern Territory, as introduced by the Federal Government in 2007, described in Chapter 1, which was directed at addressing what were considered to be 'disproportionate levels of violence'; or, for example, the standing down of child protection workers in a remote Queensland town (McLeish, 2017), which highlight the more severe consequences of these tensions. Such dilemmas are likely to arise, we argue, in the work of social workers, health professionals, teachers, police officers, doctors, community corrections workers, and other human service practitioners. We now explore these major challenges and potential opportunities.

In social work fields such as child protection, youth justice, or mental health, the mandated role (in statutory practice) is less well known in the general community, and thus the potential dilemmas are more covert. When such roles are performed in smaller communities, these issues become intensified. For example, boundaries are often blurred between practitioner as a local parent at the school and the child protection social worker. Thus, relationships in local communities are characterised by increased overlaps and dense complex social networks.

Working with so-called 'involuntary clients' can be viewed along a continuum. Intervention to remove a child at risk is an extreme example at one end, whereas imposing a court direction to encourage a young person to participate in a drug rehabilitation program allows for a wider range of intervention approaches (Trotter, Rooney & Dewberry-Rooney, 2020). In rural communities, however, these examples are often more visible and therefore more contentious. Anonymity for the client and the worker can sometimes be impossible, and maintaining confidentiality requires a higher level of scrutiny and care. Members of rural communities can be highly judgmental and have strong entrenched opinions on some issues. As an example, at the time of writing, the newly elected conservative Queensland government has legislated that offenders as young as 10 will serve adult prison terms under 'Adult Crime: Adult Time'.

We conclude here that, unlike urban settings where the worker operates at a distance, with clear professional boundaries and no personal connections to the client, rural contexts are far more complex and therefore create more complications for statutory work. We now turn to an approach to practice that does offer some opportunity for potential within rural settings.

7 Technology and innovation

In the previous chapter, we discussed how Australia is both a vast but largely urbanised (along its coastline) country. This challenge has resulted in some remarkable and unique responses. For example, the Royal Flying Doctor Service (RFDS) was formally established in 1927 with philanthropic bequests. At that time, flying light planes was still quite risky, but the alternative to rapid medical assistance was many days by horse and cart or primitive automobiles across dusty dirt roads. The RFDS became a model for other geographically challenged countries (for more details, including how early pedal-operated generators were used to power radio receivers, see Royal Flying Doctor Service (2024) https://www.flyingdoctor.org.au/about-the-rfds/history/ Accessed: 12th November 2024.)

Over twenty years ago, we highlighted how our research was exploring the ways in which new technologies were changing rural practice and rural communities more broadly (Chenoweth & Stehlik, 2002). A more recent response has been the embrace of the promise of digital technologies in communication and service delivery. The use of telehealth in medical consultations and monitoring of pathology and scans via online real-time communication platforms over the past two decades has improved access for rural communities to GPs and remote specialists. Telehealth, as it is generally termed, encompasses a range of digital technologies. This includes communication via internet platforms and mobile phone networks, as well as smart devices that record and monitor physical health information that can be relayed promptly to a distant emergency department.

While telehealth, in its various forms, has been utilised for well over 20 years, its application in social services has been slower. Nevertheless, social workers in rural areas now provide face-to-face online assessments, information giving, and counseling. They use digital platforms for connection with clients, keeping records, and reporting to the central office, which is either in the capital city or in Canberra, the federal capital. This activity increased rapidly during the COVID-19 pandemic when governments provided additional funding for these technologies as a response to lockdowns.

Certainly, these technologies have been a useful resource for people in rural communities and social workers, enabling prompt and regular communication, and, in particular, in responding to crises. Contacts that previously might have involved a two-hour drive can now be done from one's office on a laptop. However, the promise of digital technologies has not been fully realised to date, with several blind spots or gaps in their application and uptake (Warr, Luscombe & Couch, 2021).

The first is the availability of Wi-Fi and mobile networks to access these platforms, with much of rural Australia not covered by Wi-Fi or mobile networks, and access to 4G or 5G confined to towns. Drive a half a kilometre out of town, and the network drops out. Earlier last year, on a trip to central Australia and far western parts of Queensland, Lesley experienced this reality.

> It was possible to drive for 300 to 400 km with absolutely no access to a mobile network. As we approached a small hamlet, I was hopeful that we would get access at least to a mobile network to check messages or email, only to find that there was no coverage. In one instance, having driven approximately 700 km over dirt roads to arrive at a cattle station (ranch) that had indicated there was mobile coverage, I found no signal at all. The network available was for only one provider company – not the one I had! We had to drive an additional 2 1/2 hours to get mobile coverage. (Lesley).

A second blind spot is the reality of the digital divide in rural areas. The digital divide refers to a range of barriers to access and use of digital technologies. The first is reduced access to the digital infrastructure, i.e., the networks, as outlined in the example above, or the actual hardware, for example, phones, laptops, and computers, etc. Recently, the 3G network was turned off in Australia, leaving many people without any access, despite several years' warning. Another level of digital disadvantage refers to a range of circumstances that limit a person's capacity to use the technology and benefit from it. These second-order barriers are associated with socioeconomic factors, cultural reasons, or generational issues. For example, people may not have sufficient income to purchase a phone or pay for expensive data. Satellite phones are available, but the cost remains prohibitive for most people and certainly prohibitive for social work practitioners unless the job provides it. Clients, on the other hand, would have little or no capacity to use such technologies. Others who are aging, have hearing loss, or an impairment may not be able to use the available technology. For example, many First Nations Australians live in rural and remote areas and experience high levels of hearing loss (AIHW, 2024 https://www.indigenousshpf.gov.au/measures/1-15-ear-health Accessed: 24th November 2024). Such barriers then require additional investment in solutions to improve access.

In summary, digital technologies have much to offer rural and remote communities. There have been significant improvements in access and service delivery; however, real and ongoing investment in digital infrastructure should remain a top priority for rural Australia.

8 Conclusions

This chapter has outlined a brief history of rural and remote practice in Australia and how distance and lack of population have shaped the way in which human service delivery was minimal until around the late 1970s. Since then, while there has been an investment in service delivery, rural Australia still feels less connected to mainstream services and finds it more necessary to make decisions about their health, their education, and their lifestyle based on where they are located.

We have described, from our research, how the rural/remote social worker has many experiences and attributes that then determine whether they stay in place or leave, sometimes quite rapidly. Recruiting professionals to work in locations distant from cities is expensive, both financially and emotionally. Often, positions are vacant for some considerable time, adding to the locals feeling that they 'aren't that important.'

We have identified some ways in which the training of social workers and their studies can be better aligned so that when decisions are taken about where they will work, they are made with full disclosure and appreciation. There should be no 'shocks to the system' when a newly graduated social worker arrives in a local rural community.

This chapter has also drawn out the amplification of many aspects of social work practice, stemming from being part of a place and community as well as working in it. Many social workers we have worked alongside demonstrate extraordinary capabilities that are a product of both their training and their experience. They are true examples of the creative power of place and community.

This creativity and the innovative strategies that emerge from it form the substance of the next chapter.

Reflections from your experience

You have been allocated a rural placement for your final year practice placement in a small community centre 200 km from your university. There is some funding to support your experience. Think about your own experiences of rural communities, if any. What pre-placement preparation might you undertake? What kind of knowledge might you draw upon? What kinds of supports would you consider helpful? Who would you call on to help you decide?

3
The 'paradox' of community

Learning objectives

- Reflect on the paradoxical nature of 'community'
- Critically examine 'community care' and its local rural impact
- Explore the role of community development as a strategy in rural social work

1 Introduction

'Community' can be understood as a portmanteau word; that is, it has come to mean many things to different people. Despite the fact that when using it, we tend to assume we are all agreed on its definition.

We are probably also likely to believe that everyone just 'knows' what community is and that we too will know it when we see it. But is it something visual? Or something more sensual? In other words, can we feel it when it is there? Or not, if it is absent? What defines 'community'? Rather, we should ask: who defines community? The 'who' here may be people who don't actually live in that place.

These are complex questions that we will tackle in this chapter. We do so in two ways: by drawing on the expertise of those who have considered these questions (our literature) and also from our own experiences as we worked and visited many different communities, here in Australia and overseas. As a complex topic, it offers a real opportunity to you, our reader, to read beyond this chapter and delve into some of the insightful explorations of this fascinating topic.

2   Defining 'community'

The framework for our paradoxical consideration of community includes the pragmatic (but often misguided) role of governments. For any government, using a word such as 'community' gives us a powerful yardstick by which to measure their approach and its underlying ideology. Plant, Lessler, & Taylor-Grooby warn us that the term is ' … used to give an air of consensus that evaporates once the inherently normative structure of the concept is realised …' (1980, p. 207). A consequence of this vagueness can be observed in the many unfounded assumptions that are made about communities. One example is that they enshrine certain shared values. Another is that they have a shared interest, and therefore cooperation within communities is natural, normative, and usual.

One way to understand this better is to consider just who is 'in' and who is 'out' of the government's 'community'. Who is not included tells us much about who is. In Australia, a popular shorthand in these discussions is the acronym NIMBY (not in my backyard): used to describe those within who are challenging those without. As we write this (2025), the nation is considering the impacts of fossil-fuelled climate change with some arguing for a possible nuclear energy future, while others are very clear this will not happen in their backyard. In this way, community becomes a powerful tool in public rhetoric, thereby becoming and remaining constructed and re-constructed. There is also the community of experience: those who live in a particular place may not necessarily agree with the rhetorical (and often utopian) ideals put forward by others.

So just what is 'community'? We have said that it is a portmanteau word; in other words, it has come to mean whatever the writer, reader, author, or politician wants it to mean. It is a word obscured by much ideology, and by this we mean that its usage represents the set of opinions or beliefs that characterise the dominant culture. Simply put, the context of its usage can tell us much about the belief system held by the speaker/writer. In this way, 'rural community,' as we described in Chapter 2, has come to be heavily value-laden, much of it political.

The dominant ideology continues to cast it as a place in which each individual family (another portmanteau word heavy with ideology) comfortably resides, a warm, happy and harmonious place. Despite its presumed omnipresence, 'community' can be understood as essentially a hidden place. It becomes not only hard to define, but also hard to produce as evidence. It has its own camouflage, one that is of value to those wielding power. A post WW2 study found that there were 94 current definitions of 'community': their only commonality being that they all consisted of people (Plant et al, 1980, p. 204). If we were to do a similar analysis today we would likely find as many, if not more, definitions.

Just how does understanding and appreciating the ideological underpinnings of community assist the social work practitioner?

3 Social policy and community construction

Community and social policy are inextricably entwined. Social work practice, working within a social policy framework, therefore becomes the integral way in which community is both defined and operationalised. Indeed, we would argue that social workers, by their very definition, are active participants in the construction of 'community'. This can be either consciously or unconsciously. In this chapter, we will argue that as an active participant, you, as the rural social worker, should understand and appreciate the politics and paradoxes of any community in which you work. It is a truism that every community is different. There may be commonalities, but fundamentally, as you will find, they are different. In Chapter 5, we provide a framework for a strengths-based practice founded on such an appreciation.

To understand the 'history' of 'community' would require a book of its own. Briefly, with the growth of urbanisation and industralisation in the nineteenth century came a yearning to recapture a desire for the idyll associated with village life that appeared to have vanished beneath factory soot and pollution. Writers, painters, architects, and town planners led this movement, with politicians supporting it. New 'garden' towns were developed; some by philanthropists whose nearby factory gave the residents their employment. Philosophers such as Ferdinand Tönnies, when describing the vast changes his homeland of Germany was undergoing at this time, came to appreciate that the 'then' of the idyll and the 'now' of the present day had certain characteristics. He termed the 'then' gemeinschaft – meaning bonds of intimate, familial kinship and involuntary relationships; and the 'now' as gesellschaft – meaning an association brought together for a common purpose and bound only by that purpose, i.e., by work, by factory, by industry, or by social planning, as we discuss further below. These concepts have continued to dominate discussions about the nature of community.

Familial bonds and networks of connection by relationships are understood as fundamental to understanding any gemeinschaftlich community. In this analysis, what Bell & Newby (1972, p. 23) describe as 'moral custodians' can be either within the family or within churches, for example. These custodians can set the tone; they articulate the code, which community members adopt and internalise. In Australia, as elsewhere, the present-day real estate industry uses the concepts of gemeinschaft to promote not only small coastal and rural settlements but also new builds, vast suburbia on the periphery of the major capital cities. Finding your own personal 'community' has become big business here. We should ask ourselves: who are today's moral custodians?

4   Just who defines community?

Community, as a construct within social policy and practice, has both allusions and assumptions built into it: as a heavily value-laden term, it needs to be understood as representing an ideological position – one that is rarely defined, as everyone simply 'knows'. Scan any government document, and the word leaps out. It appears in legislation, in policy papers, and in social work practice standards. However, because it appears so often and in so many different ways, discovering that it is rarely defined can come as a shock.

In preparing this chapter, we explored different social work practice standards: Australia, Canada, the US, and Great Britain, and searched for the use of the word 'community' and whether it was clearly defined. In Australia, the Australian Association of Social Workers (AASW) practice standards document mentions the words community or communities four times, and it does not provide a definition, although we can read into its use its purpose as a portmanteau. First, in its opening statement:

> The AASW acknowledges Aboriginal and Torres Strait Islander Peoples, their families and communities, the First Australians, whose lands, winds and waters we all now share, and pays respect to their unique values and their continuing and enduring cultures that deepen and enrich the life of our nation and communities.

Note here that the use of 'communities' and First Nations peoples links to our argument above.

The introduction is as follows:

> Social workers operate across a diverse range of contexts, for example: working directly with individuals, families, groups and communities; conducting research and evaluation; providing education and training for future and current social workers; leading and managing public and private organisations; and contributing to policy development and implementation.

There are two standards that use the term:

Standard 4 Culture and diversity

... consult with relevant community members to inform their work with and for people from diverse identities and backgrounds.

and

Standard 9 Professional growth

Social workers are committed to maintaining and improving their practice standards through professional development. Professional growth is an ongoing process informed by the changing practice environment, new perspectives and strategies in professional domains, and changes in community expectations and outlooks (AASW, 2025).

In contrast, the Canadian Association of Social Workers (CASW) makes much more specific mention of community work, including community development and needs analysis. It provides comprehensive coverage of community development activities and interventions, as follows:

- The delivery of services and interventions that support community development and enrich individual, family, and collective well-being;
- Supervision to a social worker, social work student or other supervisors;
- The development, promotion, management, administration, delivery, and evaluation of services and programs, including those done in collaboration with other professionals;
- The management, leadership and administration of an organisation and oversight of services, programs, and interventions provided by social workers or another supervisee;

- The development, promotion, implementation, and evaluation of social policies aimed at improving social conditions and equality for individuals, families, groups, and communities, and social policies that promote social justice;
- Education, training, and professional development regarding the practice of social work;
- Research and evaluation to reflect on social work practice, to develop social policy, and to implement research-informed findings into practice, including research that engages those using social work services and research done in collaboration with other professionals.

In discussing community development, the Canadian document identifies:

- a. Analysis of community needs;
- b. Organising a community to address various social issues;
- c. Strategies that raise public awareness; and
- d. Services and interventions that support community development and community organisation. (CASW, 2025).

By contrast, the US National Association of Social Workers (NASW) offers a more field-based approach, with standards for many different domains and fields – e.g., child welfare, school social work, refugees. It details nothing specifically on community work or community development. It does provide some coverage on cultural competence, though less specific advice about interventions, skills, etc. (NASW, 2025).

In Great Britain, there are two entities that have responsibility for social work practice and standards: the British Association of Social Workers (BASW) and Social Work England. Social Work England is the regulatory body for social workers and their roles, while BASW is the professional body that supports and guides practitioners through a range of measures.

Social Work England sets out standards for what social workers need to know, understand, and do. The standards include promoting the rights, strengths, and well-being of individuals, families, and communities. This goes on to specifically acknowledge the 'differences across diverse communities' and values 'the importance of family and community systems.' (https://www.socialworkengland.org.uk/standards/professional-standards/) accessed 22nd February 2025.

BASW resources include the code of ethics, specific standards for practice educators, and a framework for quality assurance in practice learning. There are two notable inclusions of communities in the BASW code of ethics.

> Social workers should communicate effectively and work in partnership with individuals, families, groups, communities, and with public bodies and other agencies.

> Social workers should focus on the capacity and strengths of all individuals, groups and communities and thus aim to challenge stigma and promote empowerment.

(https://basw.co.uk/policy-practice/standards/code-ethics accessed 22nd February 2025)

What is of particular importance for our work is that both entities acknowledge working with strengths and the adoption of strengths-based approaches, as we discuss in detail in Chapter 5.

5 Community construction

One aspect of the overuse of the word is that it tends to homogenise individuals. It also promotes a sense of harmony, a commonality of purpose, which denies any conflict and the reality of difference; and so we continue to hear of the 'Aboriginal community', the 'Muslim community', and the 'Western Sydney community'.

A brief analysis of service provision to First Nations Australians quickly highlights the use of 'community' as a euphemism meaning 'Aboriginal' and how the struggle for the maintenance of such idealised *gemeinschaflich* environments becomes a potent force for the maintenance of the status quo. It needs restating here that for many, the 'community' in which they live was selected for them, and their resettlement there, often alongside people to whom they were not related, was determined, for them, by others. We should not ignore the social planning associated with such 'communities' and its long and sorry history, as one powerful example illustrates.

In an area of Anangu land, nearly 500 kms. north of Adelaide in South Australia, the Australian and British governments tested nuclear weapons between 1955 and 1963. Many of the local Anangu people were forcibly relocated from their traditional lands in the lead up to the tests – some were affected by the resultant fall out, which has resulted in many, many years of fighting for compensation. In late 2016, Daniela had the privilege of visiting a settlement where the descendants of some of those relocated, were now living. This settlement was on the far western margins of the desert country (spinifex country) on which the nuclear weapons testing had been carried out.

The memory of that time continues to be '… embedded right next to creation stories' (Korff, 2020) with the Alinytjara Wilurara Natural Resources Management Board (NRMB stating) that the '… living memory of this phase of our shared history casts a long shadow over any contemporary conversation …' Nuclear Fuel Cycle Royal Commission (Government of South Australia, NFCRC, 2016, p. 125).

This community, like others, is imbued with its past and as practitioners, we are obliged to understand and appreciate just how the past influences the present and present-day decision-making.

In line with other western industrialised nations, human services in Australia moved towards a market framework (with the client now called the consumer) in the early 1980s, with a series of Federal government reviews of community service programs. These reviews then changed legislation, and this in turn dramatically transformed the relationship between Federal, state, and the non-government sector. In the following decade, these changes moved towards a neo-liberalist model, where 'industry' standards developed 'benchmarks' for a wide range of issues. As a result, as we touched on in Chapter 1, what was historically a charity-based, volunteer-staffed, and often citizen-led non-government sector has over the past four decades become professionalised, corporatised, and structured to demand standards and outcomes. While this has now become normalised, it is important to learn that it was not always so and that such changes have had a marked impact on local service delivery and on the way in which the practitioner can undertake their work.

A national review of Australia's charitable (that is: non-government) organisations by the Productivity Commission of the Australian Government in 1995 identified a number of areas in which decisions regarding the restructuring of human services would influence delivery in regional, rural, and remote Australia. However, the review found that a lack of information as to the similarities and differences between the urban and regional contexts meant that the review report was limited in its response to such issues by recommending urban models and urban solutions (Australian Government Productivity Commission, 1995).

Looking back three decades, we can now see this as a vital and missed opportunity to consider place within social policy programs. This approach not only alienates the clients it is purporting to serve and diminishes their status simply because they do not live in the city, but also the professionals involved in providing the services. We return to discuss the stigma associated with being a social worker outside of urban settings in Chapter 5.

The alienation of people from the decision-making processes occurs as they become recipients of programs developed long distances from where they live, rather than active players in determining what they need. For present-day social policies, anything other than 'community' must, by definition, be secondary and undesirable. In this way, 'community care' as a human service fundamental has become heavily idealised.

Care in the community has become a truism (Clapton, 2008). It is the basis on which the majority of our current social policies are based. In Australia, over the past decades, social policy for vulnerable people has shifted from institutionalised care to 'care in the community.' However, this was not always so, as social policy once argued that such an institution actually offered the necessary care for vulnerable individuals and could be seen as a haven for those whom society had abandoned. These large conglomerate settings were often placed outside the city, in rural locations, where 'patients' engaged in farming and animal husbandry. For example, one such institution, Claremont Hospital for the Insane in Perth, Western Australia, opened in 1907 and closed in 1972. Another, the Challinor Centre in Queensland, operated as an asylum from 1933 until 1998.

Contemporary social policies continue to be founded on the assumption that it is the family (specifically, the nuclear family) where the caring of family members should be rightly conducted. It is not a surprise, therefore, to find that this construction places women at the heart of this caring role. This ideology argues that for women, either biologically or instinctively, it is 'better,' more natural, for them to care.

These ideological premises continue to lie at the heart of our welfare state, where they are in constant conflict with the reality of women in the workforce, as well as the changes the so-called 'traditional' family has undergone. While it can be seen that the pattern of work for women has changed, the assumptions about what is women's work pursue them into the paid workforce and deny them equality and justice. The juggling of roles becomes the discussion then – how much can women 'give up' in caring in order to continue to work? This conflict between ideology and reality manifests itself as a tension in the lives of women who care and creates stresses for both the caregiver and the care receiver. This conflict is one that can be said to lie at the heart of social work practice.

The assumption that the informal service sector can be relied on to provide care ad infinitum and that this will continue to 'complement' the formal service sector remains tenuous at best. The informal service sector relies on the continuing unpaid work of women in the home. In addition, it relies on the volunteer labour of women in the formal sector. The formal sector itself is ambivalent about the roles of such women. The relationship of the formal to the informal sectors and its continued tensions is a fundamental paradox of community. The invisible labour offered continues to sustain the fabric of the welfare state. Social policies tend to assume a static future. We therefore agree with Jayne Clapton (2008) that 'community care' can be best understood as an ideological euphemism, one that does not confront the underlying reality.

This assumption that lies at the heart of this euphemism is that rural communities, by their very nature, as we have discussed in the previous chapter, will be on hand to care for those needing support and will step into the gap left by diminishing or absent services. This will simply happen 'naturally' according to this assumption, as rural communities continue to be idealised as somehow 'different' from urban ones.

Social policy can be understood as fundamentally a struggle to offer equitable 'solutions' to the challenges of service delivery in rural and remote settings. We would support Plank's (1996, p. 1) assertion that a community '… that is invoked by policy analysis does not exist …' in relation to the constant and exhausting pressures to create it, or 'dream' it (as he would suggest), which becomes the responsibility of the human service practitioner to deliver. As the practitioner, you are at the boundary of place (discussed further in the next chapter) and under increasing pressure to deliver on what can be seen as utopian and, thereby, unattainable ideals. Cloke suggests that this bias towards urban-based 'one-size-fits-all' policy '… has to be continually reshaped, re-defined, and often challenged when being delivered locally …' (2006, p. 21).

In Chapter 1 we touched on how a change in the federal government in Australia in the early 1990s resulted in the withdrawal of a number of key human services from rural areas, including important services associated with caring for a family member. As the number of formal services in any geographic rural setting is, by definition, small, it can be seen that such decisions made in Canberra have huge impacts, much larger, in fact, than would be experienced in an urban setting.

The broad framework of care can be divided into four key areas: the government (both Federal and State); the commercial (or, as it is sometimes known, private-for-profit); the non-government (or voluntary, but which is actually funded by government); and finally, the informal (meaning none of the above, most likely an unpaid family member).

While the relationship between the formal and informal sectors may appear symbiotic, in fact, it has no real basis of partnership at all. In the rural context, the formal may, in fact, be very distant, either in a major centre or in a capital city. As practicing social workers, we need to be aware that, more often than not, the area of care is not perceived by policymakers in any holistic way. This, of course, reflects the neo-liberal view of the individual separate from their community. Policy tends to focus on the formal care network (and also on the commercial) sector to the exclusion of all else.

It is well beyond the scope of this book to discuss in any detail the power relationships between the formal service and the service user. However, it is important to understand that there is a power dynamic, as any human service client recognises only too soon. There is little or no empowerment in being the recipient of care services. Every social work practitioner will have a story focused on the 'non-service user'. These clients either have a lack of knowledge about what the care system can offer them or, most likely, they do know and have chosen reluctantly not to make use of them. This is often explained by the burden of care being increased through a dependency on the formal or commercial system.

The lack of knowledge of the intricacies associated with formal human services by the very people who need them and are entitled to them is a recognised challenge within the sector itself. We can take as an example here that of respite services. All too often, such 'respite' is offered as an 'in-home' service, which makes an assumption that the primary carer has somewhere to go, other than to be in their own home with her own private space – without the pressure of 'entertaining' a respite carer's presence. In the context of rural and remote respite, it really becomes a question of: where would they go?

The ongoing changes in social policy – in Australia, they tend to change at every election cycle – continue to determine whether the fabric of any 'community' can be said to withstand such impacts. We can see this as a domino effect. It has to be seen in conjunction with an ageing population, a continued fragmentation of extended families, and a constant desire by the formal service sector for 'efficiency and effectiveness'.

6 Churn in community practice

What do we mean by our term 'churn' in the context of community practice? We mean a practice climate of instability. First and importantly, it describes the common experience of vulnerable people in place and the numbers of human service professionals they are likely to have walk through their lives. While the support these many different individuals give is valuable and important, for the client, this regular change in personnel means having to 'tell their same story' over and over again. This can result in fatigue, which can lead to a lack of trust in time. If the expectation is that a client may only have a couple of visits from one practitioner and then a new one turns up, it is not surprising if the individual is less than forthcoming.

As a rural practitioner, you may enter a community where 'churn' has been the norm. It may also be a community that has a 'reputation', one that precedes it, one that you may have heard of even before arriving there. Churn assists in this construction of reputation. It can be seen as a component of the ecological framework we introduce in the next chapter. It is a negative component, however, one that will not enable flourishing. Churn is why we will spend some time in Chapter 6 discussing how to 'enter' into a rural community and also how to leave it. Entering begins long before we actually arrive in place, as we will discuss. We have an ethical responsibility to our clients when we leave a place.

Second, churn can also be applied to the transitory nature of working in a rural place. The practitioners involved – whether drawn from elsewhere or fly-in fly-out – are actively participating in maintaining the churn. It would be a salutary lesson to discover just how many practitioners have worked in a particular setting over, say, five years. Our most recent experience, drawn from the health sector, highlights that churn also plays a part in career planning. This is where the rural placement actually becomes a means to an end. The end being the achievement of a particular career goal in leaving that place and returning to the city.

Churn has a cascading effect. It creates a sense of distrust as professionals are seen as 'never local.' There is little opportunity to cross the divide if the time spent in a place is short, and we discuss this further in Chapter 5.

7 Community as social planning

We have mentioned previously how 'community' becomes a strategic initiative when social planning by governments is undertaken. A recent and powerful example of this form of social planning, which used (and abused) the term 'community,' was in the lead-up to the 2000 Sydney Olympics.

The site for the Games was chosen in inner Sydney, an area that had previously been light industrial and was less desirable as it also harbored contaminated soils. However, it was an area of housing for people who relied on government for their accommodation.

Early in the planning, some years before the Games, and in common with other previous Games cities (such as Atlanta), the clear-
ing of vulnerable people from this planned area began. Many
were relocated some 200 km north of Sydney to a small town.
During our research study of Local Area Coordination in New
South Wales, undertaken during the mid-2000s, we met some of
these residents who had been relocated. These were people with
disabilities who had no connection to this particular 'community'
and whose resettlement had been organised by the State government as part of its strategy of promoting Sydney to the rest
of the world through the Games. There was no *gemeinschaftlich*
community waiting for them, and their connections to services
were largely negotiated through service providers, including
social work practitioners. It became clear in our conversations
that while many people felt alienated from their original settings,
they did not feel at all connected to this place, as 'local' residents
expressed some resentment at their resettlement.

It is interesting to note here that, two decades later, this is still a
place where many people with disabilities live in group homes –
still largely managed through the service system. It is not too
strong to suggest that this can be viewed as a 'dumping ground'
in the so-called 'community'. We would argue that this suggests a
community presence rather than any community participation.

8 Community as geography

While this chapter has argued that community can be more than
simply geography, most social policy programs are based on
geographic principles, and none more so than those programs
being delivered beyond metropolitan settings.

Our research, undertaken in three states, tracking the introduction of Local Area Coordination (LAC), found that the issue of the borders of such programs became a crucial defining aspect of social work practice. LAC boundaries were set primarily to 'match' local government boundaries. While this may have made perfect sense in the design of the program, by possibly better enabling tidy demographic and statistical analyses, this was not the way in which local people lived and acted in place.

This point is important and therefore worth restating. The ways in which place is determined by social policy programs and management, even at a very local level, is not the way in which place is determined by those living in it. Social policies determine place in ways that 'fit' their legislative requirements, the political landscape (what party holds what seat), and access to infrastructure. Monmonier (1996) asks that we approach such planning and the maps that support them with great care. Our research found that clients simply ignored such administrative boundaries and moved around as suited them, not the program guidelines.

For example, people living in one small community (outside of the boundaries) used a town within the boundaries as their major shopping and business centre. They were naturally confused as to why they could not therefore be included in the LAC area. The issue became even more complex when LAC moved beyond Queensland into New South Wales. The two states share a border. In most people's lives, this border is imaginary, perhaps only important when there is an election or registration of motor vehicles. The LAC practitioners in New South Wales, whose borders had been determined in Sydney, found that if people had been defined as 'outside' of place, they simply travelled over the state border to Queensland and sought assistance there.

9 Does community development remain an option?

As we have previously discussed, the shift to a neoliberal approach in service delivery has meant that the strategies associated with community development have become less and less fashionable. It is critical here to note that the relationship between social work and community development has had a troubled history since the 1970s. While reaching what can be considered a high point in the 1970s, when there was real synergy between social work and social action, the rise of neoliberalism has eroded the position and importance of community work. A major factor in its decline was that community development was founded on collectivism and social action that challenges the neoliberal view that it is all about the individual.

The shifts to managerial practices, with their increasing focus on risk management, accountability, service standardisation, and performance measurement, have impacted all aspects of social work practice and driven policies and services towards individual solutions (with a fundamental argument that problems reside within individuals rather than systems), but particularly have impacted community work (see for example, Lynch, Forde & Lathouras, 2020).

This has meant that social work has moved more and more towards individual client approaches rather than broader community ones, with more focus on standardised interventions, bureaucratic reporting, marketisation, contracting out of services and monitoring, fragmentation of roles, and more technical performance. In addition, interest in community development as a strategy within the social work curriculum has also waned.

This focus sits as a real challenge for those practitioners working in communities of which they also identify as members. Indeed, O'Brien, Hawthorne-Steele, Pascoe, Moreland, Cownie, & Killick (2024) argue that this has caused a great deal of 'ethical stress' for social workers (p. 2219) as such policies and practices are at odds with core social work values. Westoby & Shevaller (2016) suggest, instead, that community development sits in a marginalised and often resistant space. However, it is noteworthy that several more recent proponents have repositioned community work as central to social work, maintaining that collective approaches are key if we are to pursue social justice and human rights. Indeed, Lathouras (2016) goes further to say it is vital that work is community-led if we are to combat exclusion and disadvantage.

10 Alliances as foundations for strengths-based practice

Earlier in this chapter, we have explained how community can also be understood as an association, or as Tönnies called it: gesellschaft.

Historically, for many practitioners in rural and remote Australia, one important connection to their discipline and to their communities-of-interest was the inter-agency framework. Membership of these networks could be eclectic, ranging from health, human services, and justice. For practitioners working alone, or in small communities, access to such inter-agency networks became a crucial professional 'lifeline'. Designed to enable 'a whole of community' approach to issues, such inter-agencies came under increasing pressure as the skills shortage and intergenerational change, as well as the neoliberal approach to focus on the individual, among other issues, took hold. In addition, inter-agency practice becomes delicately stretched when the practitioner is also a FIFO. Our research has highlighted how resourcing such opportunities can often be the first casualty when budgets are being developed, as they can be viewed as 'non-core business'. We have long supported the maintenance of interagency opportunities as being an essential component of holistic and strengths-based practice.

The emergence of Communities of Practice (CoP) offers an alternative form of workplace association. In Chapter 5 we describe just how CoPs can assist our strategies as rural social workers. This next section outlines CoP and discusses its foundational principles and how it can be utilised to support present-day *geselleschaftich* opportunities. Importantly, CoPs can also be understood as 'culturally embedded' and in that sense they form a link between the organisational workplace and the members of the CoP and their personal sense of identity. As Churchman explains (2005), these are more than likely to be voluntary associations, as individuals seek out other like-minded members to discuss issues, problems, and challenges that they have in common.

CoP emerged from within education, from what has been termed 'situated learning'. It has spread beyond teaching into business, market analysis, and of course, human services.

Stehlik, T & Carden argue that it can be a '... useful ... construct for making sense of our personal experiences of community, practice, identity, and meaning ...' (2005, p. 1). Such a construct links us not only to Tönnies but also to C. Wright Mills (1970), whom we will meet in the next chapter (personal troubles to general issues).

CoPs more broadly operate as regular discussion groups, focusing on the issues that individuals have in common. With the increasing use of digital technologies, such discussions are being held online. There is usually one individual who 'chairs' the discussion – the topic of which has been agreed upon previously. The sharing of knowledge in this way also lends itself to matters of trust and confidentiality. The ways in which others resolved issues in common become a valuable asset to the rural social worker participating in such discussions.

Most recently, we have both been involved in different forms of CoP, all within the human services and situated within large organisations (one Federal government and one non-government). This meant that they were not of the voluntary nature as described by Churchman, but rather mandated as a component of the individual's job description. This is an important difference, as it perhaps changes involvement from an active seeking of interaction and knowledge to one where membership is compulsory, activity is mandated, and therefore contributions are politically contextualised. While we support any form of communication and information sharing, our recent experiences show that it does make a difference if members actually want to be participants. The value and purpose of the CoP really only became appreciated by members well into the process. Initially, it was seen as an additional burden to their practice. Chapter 5 explains in more detail how we can incorporate successful CoP into our practice to enable a strengths-based approach.

Let us consider now the issue of alliances as fundamental to a strengths-based approach more closely. We have touched on the constant change associated with government policy, which impacts on the rural social worker and her practice. This change is not just about a change of government, although that happens with frequency; it is also about the micro-management of a particular policy to ensure that its neo-liberal framework is maintained and supported.

Over the past decades of our experience in working alongside, evaluating programs, and teaching practitioners, we have come to appreciate the power of resistance to policy as a form of practice. This can be understood as a site of struggle, where the needs of rural clients and their social work practitioners are drawn together in alliances to challenge the 'status quo' of urban-centred policies. Alongside this powerful alliance, the very geography of place makes a difference. It has become a recognised feature of practice that the further an individual practitioner is away from the 'centre' or 'head office', the more opportunities are presented to enable such challenges.

We begin this section by recounting a personal experience, one that may resonate with many practitioners. The speaker is Jean, a committed professional who has been working in rural/remote Australia for many years. She is reflecting on the way in which judgments about her work with her clients are changing. She is confused as to why this might be so. Jean explains:

We had a policy conference in Brisbane, and there were over 1,000 delegates there. What stood out to me was that if you were breaking the rules, you were seen as a 'flexible' good service, whereas for the person who [like me] sticks within the guidelines like they are supposed to, [we] come across as boring and non-innovative. We don't get anything [extra], because I run my program within the guidelines and it doesn't go over them. Let me tell you, I know people who do run outside of the [guidelines] and they get all this funding. I was told the other day, '… don't ever be good, be a little bit [naughty] don't follow the guidelines, bend the rules a bit and you may get a little bit more, because people take notice of people that bend the rules'. Or you play dumb and when they find out about you, plead innocent'.

Jean was very clear about her dilemma. She had contracted with her agency to work within the guidelines of her program: guidelines that had been developed in both Canberra and Brisbane. However, as we now understand, her clients had their needs framed within the place in which they lived, which was a smaller settlement, a long way from either city. All too often, these urban guidelines did not offer Jean the flexibility to meet that local need. They ignored the differences between urban and rural. How should she respond? How could she resist (push back) on such guidelines? Should she, ethically? If she does, what happens? It appears from her story that there may be rewards for such resistance, but is that so?

To consider this in more detail, we return to the history of social work practice, which was founded in forms of activism. A very early social work text provided a checklist for activist community practitioners (Jones, Cheever & Ficklin, 1971) and was received without controversy – it was just what social workers did. A decade later, and in the context of the growth of a neo-liberal conservative agenda, Burghardt (1982) predicted that while 'localised action' could not be ignored, its '… basic flaw is that more and more issues are tied directly to national concerns …' (p. 109). In other words, it was becoming harder to resist locally against such a national agenda.

A further decade later, and Leonard (1997) was now arguing for collective, rather than individual, resistance as more powerful against a mass commodified culture. These collectives can also be understood as alliances. We suggest that within rural social work practice lies the potential for a network of alliances between practitioners and community members that can be understood as a response or resistance to those policies which tend to disempower.

Cooper (1994) reminds us that the very concept of resistance is imbued with a notion of power; indeed it '… cannot exist in a relationship of exteriority to it …' (p. 443). This is not the heroic form of resistance – up to the barricades - this form of resistance is observable in the everyday practices of ordinary life, and practitioners can be seen as active agents within these sites of struggle.

We can link this to our discussion of community above, as the social worker actively constructs community through their practice and their activism. As a fundamental aspect of social work practice, we agree with Rein (1970) that such practice is not simply about ensuring that clients get the services they are entitled to or helping them to 'adapt' to their environment, but to encourage … individuals to alter their external circumstances as well as seeking direction to change the framework of expectation and the level of provision that are contributing to their difficulties … (Rein, 1970, p. 28).

In the next chapter, we describe how our practice can move beyond resilience towards flourishing, and Rein's point underlies this. We now describe two examples of this form of alliance building and its response to centralised power. Vicki discusses how the effect of a policy decision to close part of her local rural hospital enabled her to participate in a challenge to that decision. She describes how

> … one of the wards at the base hospital was used as a geriatric ward where people were placed waiting for a more permanent place, and also for emergency respite. That was really wonderful. At an aged care assessment meeting one day we were addressed by the hospital hierarchy and told that the wards were no longer going to be utilised in this way. The decision had been made so quickly that the community found itself without any emergency respite. Instead, they were expected to go home immediately. (Vicki).

Vicki's act of resistance? She began an informal campaign among her clients and her network to discover how such a decision could be taken without any consultation.

One of our clients [wrote to the politicians]. She was very angry and outspoken. She contacted the newspaper, a photo and everything. The response to media interest was immediate. The radio put it over and then they interviewed the State Minister for Health, who said 'there was nothing cut' and he would be 'speaking to the hospital administrator'. Then the local paper got involved with a photo of my client, and the next minute, the funding was back and the decision changed.

Vicki's tactic was to support her client with any necessary information. She did not take the lead but rather supported the community member to enable the challenge to be made publicly and to be well informed.

Another example from Sue relates to how services have become corporatised. At the interview, practitioners expressed concern that their clients were vulnerable to being exploited by, for example, being overcharged for services or being charged twice. Corporatisation and the 'user pays' principle have meant that many clients have to go to a number of agencies to get the same service. Practitioners queried, '... who do they pay, how much do they pay, and who gets the money? Who does what with it? A lot of them are on a pension; how do they afford it?' The strategy adopted by Sue was to enable the establishment of an alliance with her local service providers. She recalled that '... as we all work fairly well together, we do tend to share. Elsewhere, you might get services that don't have a good rapport with one another, and therefore they all want to be paid. We are lucky.' Alliances such as these need support, encouragement, and time to establish and maintain. They also require trust and honesty: not competition, but cooperation.

Alliances and the empowerment of clients are among the tactics being used by some practitioners as ways of resisting/challenging dominant policies that simply 'don't work' locally. Neither of these alternatives is new, as they are deeply embedded in the practice of social work as a discipline. Haynes & Mickelson (1997) cite an example from 1924 in Lindeman. Such alliances work against the powerful urge to de-communitise, a legacy of neo-liberal ideologies. This de-communitisation can be seen in the sense of loss of place and kinship (their *gemeinschaftlich* characteristics) that many individuals experience. Our research has highlighted how practitioners maintain a sense of purpose and ethics in the face of increasing pressures to compromise. We return to these important strategies again in the following chapter.

11   Practice in times of disaster

Environmental crises, such as floods, wildfires, and drought, are part of living in Australia, and living either rurally or remotely adds to this less-than-happy expectation. In the past, social work curricula have tended to elide 'disasters' as being once-in-a-lifetime experiences such as, perhaps, a cyclone. This has changed dramatically in the past two decades, as global warming speeds up and climate changes and variabilities are now lived experiences for many. This can mean that a rural social worker's experience now includes not only being actively and personally involved in such a disaster but also working alongside their community in recovery. Gray, Coates & Hetherington (2013) have tackled both these aspects of practice head-on in their groundbreaking edited collection. Without restating its many excellent contributions here, we highly recommend that as part of your preparation for working rurally and remotely, you make yourself familiar with this text and others that focus on these issues.

Our ecological framework, working from a strengths-based perspective, can come under pressure when a community and practitioner face a disaster. The bonds that tie a community together – as a *geselleschaftlich* entity – can come under threat if the disaster impacts not just on livelihoods but also on the built environment, as is the case in wild(bush)fires. Such events tend to scatter people from place, and many may not, in fact, return. Losing a home can, as Peter Read (2006) reminds us, be similar to losing a loved one. 'Do residents of farms love their places more than residents of suburbs?' he asks (p. x) and further, 'how do humans form such powerful and mysterious attachments to country?' (p. 2). He tackles both these issues head-on, with stories of places lost and destroyed and how individuals coped with that loss, in *Returning to Nothing: The Meaning of Lost Places,* as relevant today as it was twenty years ago.

There have been many disasters in Australia in the past two decades since Read's book was published, including fires that destroyed nearly 500 homes, 490 people injured, and 4 sadly died, in Canberra, the nation's capital in 2003. In 2012/2013, over 41,000 people were isolated by flooding in New South Wales, and over 75 percent of that state was under flood warnings, with forced evacuations during. Disasters, by their very nature, become political. For the social work practitioner, working within both a highly political and highly sensitive environment becomes a challenge.

A more insidious, and perhaps for that reason, less well-appreciated disaster was that of the Millennium Drought. While officially listed as lasting from 2001 to 2009, in fact, dry seasons had begun as early as 1991, and fewer dry seasons between in the subsequent decade just put off its inevitable impact. It directly affected the country's 'food bowl,' the Murray-Darling River Basin, and the dust storms and subsequent lack of water finally impacted even the major cities of the eastern seaboard. What did we learn from this experience that we can apply to social work practice? As (Daniela) wrote subsequently (Stehlik, 2013):

> Doing social work within an environmental context became a 'real-life' experience for many practitioners during the major Australian droughts of the past two decades. It is in the nature of such a crisis that social workers rarely, if ever, have an opportunity to reflect on the ways in which their practice deals with, or changes, during the crisis itself (p. 135).

The chapter goes on to detail just how the three tiers of government—Federal, State, and local—as the political nature of this disaster writ large operated during the crisis, and those social workers employed within government agencies who worked alongside affected communities. One immediate example was that of home visiting, as a strategy developed to make certain that individuals had access to up-to-date information and also to ensure that people felt they had the support they needed as the long-term nature of this drought began to visibly affect people's mental health. Not everyone could be visited, however, as once again, the tyranny of geography and distance hindered practice. States such as Victoria, more easily accessible, had more support workers available to them. States such as Queensland struggled. A subsequent report found that '… one community support worker had responsibility for an area of 700,000 sq. kms, nearly three times the size of Great Britain' (Stehlik, 2013, p. 153) with limited funding.

One critical point can be made here: the nature of the client. We are very familiar with the idea that clients of 'the welfare' are usually those most vulnerable in society, perhaps even those whose family history has been one of vulnerability. In the case of crises such as the ones discussed above, 'the client' can be someone who has never had to ask for help from a government or a non-government agency. In the case of the Millennium Drought, in fact, were it not for the crisis itself, '… the majority … would not need or seek help [as they] were not repeat users of what can be considered 'traditional' welfare assistance (Stehlik, 2013, p. 140). Recognising this fact was a critical aspect of ensuring that practice in crisis was undertaken with sensitivity and diplomacy '… as people affected by drought have an acute sense that their identity and place are under threat, their known world has been turned upside down, and there are no certainties on which to rely' (p. 140). Becoming reliant on 'the welfare' was, to many, a stigmatising experience.

We return to the impact on practice and ways in which a strengths-based approach can assist in dealing with disasters in Chapter 5.

12 Conclusions

This chapter has covered a number of critical areas of practice: what are the implications for social workers in rural communities?

First, as discussed above, much of this work will inevitably create dilemmas and tensions. Being part of communities seeking to address critical problems, and often themselves being part of those communities, places the practitioner in that wedged space between operating within government policies that construct human problems within the individual, and yet having the knowledge and values that would see community approaches as critical to facilitate inclusive engagement and address power imbalance aspects that are crucial for many rural and remote communities.

Second, it has become apparent that many newer graduates have not had significant focus on community work or community development in their training. While Cheryl, whom we met in the previous chapter, spoke glowingly about her social work studies and the extensive focus on community theory and skills she experienced in the late 1970s, many present-day programs simply do not include this in-depth or only offer brief and cursory attention. This places the practitioner in a difficult situation for which they are not fully equipped.

This was evident too in the omission or passing mention of community work in the practice standards comparisons earlier in this chapter. This is an international problem. For example, O'Brien et al. (2024) highlight the need for investment in community development in social work programs in Northern Ireland. Lathouras and colleagues (2016) also argue this case for Australia, while Turbutt & Pye (2024) from the UK suggest that rural social work content in the curriculum needs to be rebuilt from the ground up.

Our next chapter offers a framework for rural practice that takes into consideration many of the issues we have discussed.

Reflections from your experience

Go to your government webpage that focuses on community. This might be national, regional, or your local authority.

In what ways is community described?
Has it been defined?

From reading this, what kind of communities are talked about? Who is missing?

4

The power of 'place':Place-identity as a strategy for strengths-based ecological practice

Learning objectives

- Illustrate how place shapes identity
- Explore how an understanding of place is important for rural social work practice
- Articulate how strengths-based practice can be enabled within an ecological framework

1 Introduction

In this chapter, we propose an alternative approach to the currently dominant, ideologically constructed views about living and working in rural Australia. We do this from a practitioner-led perspective.

We have touched on place as a critical aspect of practice in previous chapters. Here we introduce a (re)imagining of rural practice founded on the concept of place identity and grounded in a form of praxis. We build on concepts developed by (among others) Chris Cuomo (1998) and C. Wright Mills (1970), as well as evidence from our own research undertaken with rural practitioners. This has led us to conclude that there is a potential for resistance that enables strengths-based practice. We also take the concept of community resilience beyond that of simply 'bouncing back' toward a community that is flourishing.

The next section offers a brief outline of what is meant by the terms we use.

In previous chapters, we have detailed the challenges and barriers associated with working as a practitioner in rural settings. Here, guided by the teachings of C. Wright Mills (1916–1962), an American sociologist who coined the term the sociological imagination, wherein our personal troubles can be seen as directly connected to social issues (Sargent 1995, p. 2), we ask the following critical question, as posed by Mills: How could it be otherwise? How could the dominant framework be otherwise – as an asset rather than as a liability – as a positive rather than a negative – not as a deficit but as a credit? How can our practice within and with rural communities take us beyond resilience toward flourishing?

We begin this (re)framing or foundational (re)construction by drawing on various theoretical approaches. These offer some alternatives to the dominant discourses and powerful ideologies as previously discussed. We suggest that these can provide us with the confidence and strength essential to mounting a non-deficit-laden alternative for you (the practitioner) to draw on.

2 Flourishing as a framework

We can call our framework having an ecological perspective. This is built on the groundbreaking work of C. J. Cuomo (1998): Feminism and Ecological Communities. An Ethic of Flourishing. Cuomo asks us to consider that we understand our society and the communities that it supports in a way that continues to allow us to '… negotiate our personal, social, and institutional relationships … '(1998, p. 4). This ecological approach offers us

> … ways of thinking, and of evaluating actions, policies, and values that challenge destructive and oppressive modes of interaction, and that encourage deep thought and carefulness in the face of lies and illusions … (1998, p. 5).

We can also think of these 'lies and illusions' as being the myths and ideological concepts about 'the rural' that we have discussed elsewhere.

An ecological understanding offers us an essential aspect of our reinterpretation of the current state of rural Australia, of the people who live and work and have their sense of identity associated with rural place (see further below) and who are experiencing rapid changes in lifestyle and associated well-being. By adopting an ethic of flourishing within an ecological perspective, we recognise how human beings need both connection and community for their continued well-being.

Flourishing as a framework is critically important as it occurs 'in process' during change, and therefore can only be viewed and understood in hindsight. In this sense, Cuomo builds on the need for a historical perspective (also drawing on C. Wright Mills) to our analysis of societal issues. Flourishing can only be determined 'over the long haul' by drawing on not just science, but 'other sources of wisdom, including oral traditions, narratives, and practical insight' (1998, p. 78). Cuomo argues that we can only really begin to appreciate the richness, depth, and potential of human flourishing through

> ... contextualized, ... local, evaluations of what it means to be human, what people want and strive for, and what enables their living in ways they value in specific historical and cultural locations ... (p. 79).

Cuomo therefore offers us a nuanced view of the human condition, enabling a deeper appreciation the more commonly used concept of 'resilience'. How is this so? Flourishing implies a future, a striving for connection, but one morally central to the perspective of those who live in place. It also implies learning, preparing, and taking control of our lives – having agency. In this way it enables us to consider how our practice can contribute to community flourishing.

In previous chapters, we have touched on the decades of change and their associated challenges for rural communities in Australia. In considering these in hindsight, as Cuomo asks us to do, highlights the paucity of an ethic of flourishing associated with places outside of the metropolitan, and just how few (either state or Federal) government policies over the past decades have enabled any transition toward a flourishing future: on the contrary.

This leads us to ask: can a practitioner work towards a flourishing future within their rural community? Indeed, can one individual achieve anything against the power of the current ideological framework? We made the point in the previous chapter that social workers, by their very definition, are active participants in the construction of community. Working within rural communities offers a direct prospect to our ability to work alongside others, intimately and over time. It gives each of us an opportunity to make a difference.

This intimate work impacts how others see their place in the world, enabling paths to follow and providing opportunities for choice to participate in the wider world, suggesting how, as a practitioner, you can also be a guide or a teacher. A foundational philosophy of education is useful to consider here as we would argue that all educators need to view themselves

> … as part of a cluster of professional roles providing an integrated and holistic contribution to education that goes beyond the classroom and school to the wider community … (T. Stehlik, 2018, p. 11).

This is the potency of place and practice: praxis. You, as a practitioner, are central to the concept of an ecological community and therefore essential for its future flourishing. For the professional practitioner, this critical role means '… developing good relationships … with clients; it also, more importantly, means actively striving against the dominant discourses, through '… contextualizing their lives, [and] not having unrealistic assumptions about their family lives and expectations ..' (2018, p. 164).

Arriving in a rural community with the baggage of assumptions and stereotypes based on some perceived 'agreed' mental picture we may have of the people and their lives does not enable an ethic of flourishing. In fact, it is unlikely to do so. This mental picture encompasses their relationships with others, their connection to their wider environment, and their sense of self and identity to this place. In fact, such assumptions will do the very opposite and will work against an ethic of flourishing. We are continuing to support the deficit structure of an ideological framework that actually diminishes lives and potential futures. Everything you see, everything you hear, will reinforce, either positively or negatively, this pre-determined mental picture.

Where to start to explore this further? First, let us consider the daily language we use when we communicate with others in our community, and then let's move beyond language and into action. This will then link us to another aspect of our ecological framework: that of a place-based and strengths-based approach.

3   Praxis in place

A strengths-based approach (SBA) does not ignore any challenges; on the contrary, it values the '… capacity, skills, knowledge, connections and potential in individuals and communities …' (Pattoni 2012, p. 1). 'Connections' is emphasised here because it links us back to Cuomo's concept of an ecological framework. The rural professional is not alone. There is a whole community associated with the work they undertake. There is the service community, the broader community of practitioners (Ewing, 2008) – which may or may not be locally based – a community of ideas, and then, powerfully, the geographic community in which they live and work.

Building a practice from a strengths-based perspective enables you to draw on this collaboration in a very positive, affirming way by 'embracing' an 'asset-based approach,' which in turn argues '... against the dominance of a problem-focused perspective ...' (Pattoni, 2012, p. 2). This means that working within a rural setting, and putting the rural first, suggests that there is a strength associated with that decision, a powerful statement about the resources available, and a recognition that this place is valuable and that the people who live here do form a vital and contributing part of Australian society.

We demonstrate this most powerfully through the language we use to speak about this community, our clients, their families, and their aspirations and struggles. Earlier, we explained how an ecological community supporting an ethic of flourishing relies on wisdom from other sources such as oral traditions, narratives, and practical insights. SBA can support a narrative-based strategy to better appreciate and support the strengths within a community or an individual. In this way, the

> ... practice of narrative is founded on the principle that people live their lives by stories or narratives that they have created through their experiences, and which then serve to shape their further life experience ... (Pattoni, 2012, p. 5).

Such narratives (stories, yarns, and anecdotes) are familiar to anyone who has lived and worked in rural Australia or any rural setting. They speak to connections, to memory, to historical events, to the relationships between people and animals, between people in this place, and to other places. By careful listening, the rural practitioner can distinguish within this narrative the strengths and capacities of individuals and, by extension, their community. We speak of 'connecting the dots' – in this way of listening we are actively involved in detecting and connecting the dots of strengths, drawing on them, and thereby creating a powerful challenge to the deficit discourses as we do so. For one client, her relationship with her LAC, who was also local, was based on trust and deliverables:

> … if you want to find something out [LAC] knows who to get on to. And you just get on to them. … And all that stuff that no one knows. She kinda knows … She can tell you who to get on to … For years here no one told you nothing. The only ones I was getting around was from P. (service). They'd come around once a year and they'd tell you stuff, but they didn't know much about …[things] round here. It was all in Brisbane. You had to get it done in Brisbane …

Two examples from our own experiences highlight these important aspects. The first comes from Canada, where our participation in a rural practice conference in Lethbridge, Alberta, gave us the opportunity to take up an invitation to visit a Hutterite community nearby. The members of this community were keen to explain to their international visitors how the community managed to hold their values and principles in the face of twenty-first-century impacts. We learned that the rural lifestyle within a small communal setting meant that each community has between 90 to 150 members. In Alberta, the 2016 census recorded some 138 of these colonies. (Canadian Encyclopedia, 2019 at https://www.thecanadianencyclopedia.ca/en/article/hutterites Accessed: 3rd January 2025).

Families lived in houses that were traditionally built, and we visited the school and shared kitchen. As an example of a community and place that was completely different from anything we had previously experienced, it was a memorable visit. One aspect, contrary to previously held assumptions, was their use of high-tech farming equipment and their relationship with the local urban and rural communities around them. In fact, in contrast to our assumptions, they were not cut off from their neighbours.

Lesley was fortunate enough to be included in a study visit to Inuit communities in northern Canada. Nunavut is a remote and sparsely populated territory comprised of an administrative centre, Iqaluit, and a number of very small remote villages. The delivery of services is primarily based on a fly-in fly-out model that we discuss further in the Australian context below. Many health services involve patients being flown south for treatment. It was a long flight to major cities. For many pregnant women living several hours by air from tertiary maternity hospitals, this meant being transferred to Ottawa, Montréal, or Toronto to deliver their babies. This meant being several weeks away from home, their families, and their other children.

Remote communities such as these rely almost entirely on government services. At the time Lesley visited, Nunavut was at the halfway point of a 20 agreement with the Canadian government, which aimed to create economic development for the Territory in return for a grant for those communities over the 20 period. With a population of some 26,000 people, these services, which included health, child welfare, and education, were coordinated and delivered from the capital, Iqaluit. Remoteness also meant that the cost of living was extremely high for everyone living there. The general store, also government-run, provided non-local food at exorbitant prices and also included fast food options that were only marginally cheaper. We heard that the capacity to hunt and provide food through traditional Inuit practices was shrinking. Some of this was due in part to the loss of ice (a direct impact of global warming) as a means of transport, and we also heard of several tragic deaths where hunters on snowmobiles perished through the thinning ice. Inuit communities were also facing growing pressure from the influx of resource sector personnel, exploring for mining opportunities and other natural resources.

It soon became apparent that there were many parallels with our work in the remote communities of far north Queensland and Western Australia. The isolation and vast distances with inaccessible roads for a great part of the year in these Australian regions have many similarities with remote icebound communities beyond the Arctic Circle, which were reliant on air travel, with some access in the summer by ship.

We have also been struck by the similarities of these remote communities culturally. Inuit communities historically had experienced the impact of colonisation, albeit much later than in other countries. It had been assumed that there were no readily accessible natural resources in their lands on offer, whereas Australian Indigenous communities were impacted from the earliest settlement in the late eighteenth century, as we have described previously. For both, the relationship to place is similarly central and deeply held. For Inuit, staying 'on the land' was crucial to their very being, and for Indigenous Australians, knowing and acknowledging the land of one's ancestors and visiting one's traditional 'country' is similarly inextricably bound together with identity and being.

4 Narratives of place

One of the greatest strengths human beings have to draw on is their sense of identity: of who they are. The personal identities of your clients and their families are firmly based in a sense of place. We have touched on this several times previously. Here we want to explore this further and offer it as a third aspect of an alternative framework in our search for (re)valuing rural Australia.

What is meant by place in this context? It is much more than simple geography; indeed, it can transcend it. For Casey (2001), place is connected to the landscape through our bodily experiences. Dale-Hallett, Diffey, O'Keefe & Wilson (2008, p. 45) suggest that place can be defined by the 'social relationships surrounding an event' and such events offer opportunities for 'social action and change' to be fostered. These events can be formally organised or informal gatherings. Many rural and remote communities have become defined by such events beyond their local residents, to a broader audience. Festivals, rodeos, and country shows are all opportunities to reconnect with place identities. Place can be political, spiritual, social, cultural, or historical. Place is also gendered and is influenced by variables such as age, ethnicity, and culture. A sense of place, as Vanclay reminds us, is

> ... the contemporary everyday connection individuals have with their local spaces that gives their life meaning in the present ... [and] ... place exists when the individual can tell a story about a specific locality, something

that indicates personal meaning. … Places exist when we start naming them (2008, p. 4).

An Indigenous woman describing her local community powerfully amplifies this point as follows:

I was brought up with that mountain that river is our boundaries. Dad was from the southern side of the river and mum was from the northern side of the river … of course, there was a lot of intermingling of blood line [at town A] so you had a crew over from [town B] at that's the [town C] area, the … people … the people.

Place attachment can be understood in a variety of ways: through history or family lineage; through the loss of land or destruction of community; the mourning of things lost, as Read (1996) outlines. Place attachment can be understood through land ownership or inheritance; through spiritual or mythological celebratory events; and through narrative linkages, such as storytelling and place-naming. It follows then that listening to the stories of place can be seen as a key by which you may be able to get 'inside' your community.

A personal experience highlights this relationship between place, praxis, and identity. We have described how Western Australia is one of Australia's largest states, with a small population mostly centred around the capital city, Perth. This means that living in rural or remote settings is a challenge, but even more so if the family has a child with a disability. The early years can be a roller coaster of meetings with doctors, specialists, allied health professionals, and others. All of these services are located in Perth, and until very recently, any travel to meetings had to be a long trip to the city, undertaken by the parents, or perhaps more often, by the mother. In the early 1990s, the Western Australian government trialed a radical program of service delivery to people with a disability in their own homes. It particularly focused on those living beyond the metropolitan area. It was a pilot program – called Local Area Coordination (LAC) – and it was introduced with a formative evaluation program working alongside the practitioners. As a member of the LAC evaluation team, Daniela was able to visit some of those families whose lives had changed because the practitioners came to them, rather than the other way around. She has always remembered these visits, as they were powerful lessons on the way in which families cared for their loved ones in the face of the challenge of a disability. In particular, one such visit taught her a useful and remarkable lesson about 'community.'

Let's look at a map of Western Australia, starting with Perth and moving eastwards. Eventually, we find a structure on the map called 'the rabbit proof fence.' Constructed at the turn of the twentieth century, it stretches from the south coast to the north coast over some 1800 kms. This is 'wheatbelt' country, the area the early European colonists changed forever from bush to grain-growing – hence the need to keep out rabbits. The 'farms' here are very large (many hectares), and crops other than wheat are now also grown. Settlements are few and far between, mostly centred around the major roads. Fewer than 150,000 people live in the Wheatbelt, across an area of some 155,000 sq. kms - or one person per square km.

Driving through this landscape on her way to visit a family who lived 'beyond the rabbit proof fence' was certainly a challenge before the era of sat. navs. After some 4 hours, Daniela finally came to a small settlement (petrol station), and from there made her way to the farm where she was to meet Mary and her new baby. During the interview, over tea and scones, with her baby sleeping in her stroller, Mary talked about her 'community' and how they had all rallied around her and her husband following the birth of her baby girl.

Where was this community? Daniela asked in her ignorance, thinking it was some larger settlement that she appeared to have missed in her drive to the farm. My neighbours, she replied, they live all around here, and we meet at the local tennis court. You would have passed it on your way here. Where is it? Daniela asked. Next to the petrol station!

On her way out, Daniela went to the petrol station (several kms from the farm) again. This time she saw it through Mary's eyes. There was the tennis court. There were the seats where she and her neighbours sat together. Mary's 'community' was geographically as widespread as it could only be in Western Australia, but to Mary, these distances made no difference as she felt connected and close to her neighbours. 'Community is certainly much more than geography' was the lesson I took away that day' (Daniela).

Our personal sense of identity is complex, and we often act it out in unconscious ways. Active listening is, therefore, crucial. You may be from elsewhere; indeed, it is likely that you are from somewhere else (another place), but in listening to the local stories, the oral traditions, the histories and memories of those around you, you will be honouring not only their sense of place but your own. As this understanding deepens, it...

> … forces an acknowledgement of the social, cultural, historical, and political flows that constantly reshape places, as well as the people and power structures that operate within them (Ardoin, 2006, p. 118).

This awakening to the politics of place is crucial if the challenge in offering an alternative approach to practice is to be successful. In our LAC research, we found that for many people the practitioner was their only contact with the state government. From the standpoint of a person living remotely, understanding government roles and responsibilities, is, to say the least, daunting.

In summary, our alternative approach that works towards (re)valuing the rural offers an ecological framework based on a strengths-based practice deeply located in place. Drawing this framework together is the concept of praxis. Praxis (understanding theory through practice) denotes a sense of agency, a critical aspect of our alternative approach. Agency implies that there is the potential for human action. This action draws on the strengths within us and around us, and it enables us to act in the world. From an ecological perspective, such agency is drawn from others around us. We are not alone. This agency can also be viewed historically.

Place attachment and place identity have been challenged through policies that have elided and diminished what it means to live in rural Australia (Stehlik, 2017). Consequently, we can now observe how place attachment and place identity are increasingly becoming markers of resistance to the dominant, urban-centric discourses that frame the current ideology of rural Australia. This resistance can be observed through the activities of practitioners more broadly and their decisions to work rurally.

5 The politics of praxis in place

We have stated several times that the practitioner works within a political context and that being located outside of the metropolitan area can be both a strength (far away from the centre) and a weakness (information takes time to arrive).

In our earlier study of human service practitioners we identified a trend towards having to deal with 'policy on the run', as well as reversals of accepted modes of practice. These are most often experienced following elections, but they can also be a result of a particular interest by a Minister or from sustained media interest. A most recent, relevant and potent example occurred in Queensland following the October 2024 state election that saw a change of government to a conservative coalition. Following extensive community consultation, the previous government had established a Truth-telling and Healing Inquiry that had just commenced its public hearings (Government of Queensland, 2024). The election was held on 26th October, 2024 and just over a month later, on 28th November, with little warning, the new government abolished the Inquiry that had just commenced its 3 year term, and removed Inquiry Members from office. A statement from the Inquiry about this decision can be read at:

https://www.truth-telling-qld.com.au/final-statement-truth-telling-and-healing-inquiry (Accessed: 28th January 2025).

When such changes are made in haste, these policies do not follow the traditional pathway of consultation with the community, of the bureaucracy offering expert advice, but instead are influenced and directed by individual views, through ideologies, or as strategies to 'solve' a perceived media issue. For human service personnel in rural and regional communities, where the distance from the speaker and the enactor is far greater than their urban counterparts—who are themselves also distanced as they have not been consulted—this affects their ability to do their work effectively. Alongside this trend is another, as formal consultation and advisory processes that previously informed policy development are increasingly being dismantled. Community consultation is promoted as being 'old-fashioned,' something that has been done once and does not have to happen again. A more 'immediate' and less costly approach is perceived as that offered through social media and also by talkback radio—apparently, this reaches a broader audience. Gathering the concern of the wider and local constituency has become less fashionable.

The social work practitioner can assist their community in promoting its views on policy changes through what we have termed 'resistance.' For example, in the late 1990s, two street marches protesting the halting of Institutional Reform were organised in Brisbane, and in the same year, a group of families with relatives living in institutions formed a lobby group to agitate and pressure for policy change. A masked group of staff from various human service agencies protested in public about the abuses that occur in such institutions. On these occasions, practitioners played an important role.

A 3-year study we conducted with a grant from the Australian Research Council, during which 800 professionals (nursing, social work, education, and police) working in rural and remote Queensland were surveyed (Jervis-Tracey, McAuliffe, Klieve, Chenoweth, O'Connor & Stehlik, 2016), will give us some understanding of the motivations associated with the decisions to build such resistance. Our study found that recruitment and retention of professionals (as we outlined in Chapter 2) are very much influenced by place, as well as by the actual physical nature of the job and its workload. Any decisions to challenge the status quo within practice are not taken lightly, as there is a degree of activism associated with them, whereby the practitioner understands that in doing so, they actually become an advocate for place specifically, and 'the rural' more broadly. In other words, the motivation to work outside of urban settings comes with an appreciation of this fact; perhaps if not immediately understood, one learns it fairly quickly. This finding is critical in a deeper understanding of both place and agency. Most of the services delivered in non-urban settings are predominantly managed from urban settings—often quite distant. Therefore, an urban bias can be read not only within the language used to determine policies, programs, curriculum, and so forth but also in the flow-through of decisions and actions. This bias, then, has to be reshaped, redefined, and often directly challenged when being delivered rurally by the individual practitioner or groupings of individuals.

Our rural or remote practitioner works at the perceived 'periphery'—a fact that may often feel as being 'outside the mainstream' or 'forgotten'. We suggest that the periphery can be a site of resistance, and it can also be leveraged as a powerful aspect of agency. How the practitioner works within these dominant discourses, how they advocate for and enable place identity, and support those they serve can be seen as tactics within a form of everyday practice. The further we are away from the centre, the more capacity and space we possess to initiate and maintain resistance to any dominant discourses by the use of active and positive language.

Such spatial freedom can be undertaken locally and personally. In some cases, it can be liberating. In others, it can be stressful. This anxiety could be attributed to a sense of being alone in this struggle. Being a solitary advocate is not easy. However, an ecological framework, drawing on a strengths-based perspective, gives promise that we work within alliances that are a powerful way of challenging the 'despatialisation' that our current urban-centric policies demand. Being a member of such an alliance (virtual as well as physical) can give both hope and courage, as well as help us to maintain the energy necessary for the ongoing challenge.

The traditional human service model of being 'distanced' from the community in which a practitioner works is being challenged by approaches for rural and remote communities where practitioners are very much part of their community and have dual relationships across professional and private spheres of life. For example, one may be working as a practitioner with a person who may be the local shopkeeper or on the local parents and teachers group. The blurring of roles of being a practitioner and local community citizen can create conflict. This is not an uncommon phenomenon and can be understood as a tension between the needs and ways of the local community and the demands and requirements of a centrally based formal organisation. Research indicates that human service workers living in rural and regional communities are more likely to identify and be aligned with their community over their organisation (Chenoweth & Stehlik, 1999; Martinez-Brawley, 2000).

This also touches on another critical aspect of working in place: that of personal identity and loyalty. In our work with Local Area Coordinators (LACs), the issue of identity and loyalty as a member of the community or as a government employee emerged. LAC principles were based on them being a member of the community first and as a bureaucrat second. This was observed as a tension within the program and developed as a real dilemma for LAC practice. Indeed, we found that it ultimately led to a reduction of the program across the state. This autonomy held by the practitioner did not last. It was cut back as a result of withdrawing the small amount of discretionary funds they had previously held. It therefore is important that social work practitioners understand how the 'borders' (either real or imaginary) of their practice operate. Borders can be useful, as for example, ensuring that those in need also understand the borders of the social policy programs that affect them. In our work, we met practitioners who actively challenged these borders in order to meet a pressing need for clients just outside the border.

For the social worker arriving in their 'new' community, the determination of borders is a crucial step in their 'entry plan'; some aspects of which can already be undertaken while still at head office or before starting in the position; others will emerge as their appreciation of the community strengthens.

The context in which the rural practitioner works and lives is central to building an alternative position of the value of rural Australia in future decades. Understanding these contexts is critical, as they are 'consequential, not incidental' and enable us to appreciate the '.. variability in child, family, school, and community outcomes … [and consequently how] place-based uniqueness needs to become a priority' (Lawson, 2016, p. 14).

6 Changes in praxis

We have spent some time explaining just how important place is to our social work praxis. How does this then fit with the increasing trend towards a fly-in fly-out (FiFo) model of care? This has become an increasingly important characteristic of the neoliberal marketised approach to human services as they are currently delivered in rural and remote Australia. Initially established within the mining sector to resolve issues of workforce accessibility, it has now become a more common approach in our larger states.

We explained in Chapter 1 that as the cost of accommodation in remote Australia increases, and the capacity of small communities to provide the breadth of education and cultural attractions necessary for a highly skilled and demanding workforce diminishes, the trend towards a FiFo approach to service delivery seems highly opportune, and, on the numbers, probably economically more efficient. However, it comes at a cost, not only to the client whose experiences of such services are fragmented, hit-and-miss, and lack continuity; but also to the professionals who visit, who become disassociated from their clients and do not have the time or the energy to move 'outside' of the workplace to connect with people beyond their practice. The National Rural Health Alliance (2013) has called this a 'conundrum'; in other words, that there is an 'inherent conflict between distance and equity' in providing services to Australians who live in remote communities.

This reshaping of work through FiFo in order to enable access to resources and provide services to remote Australia has, over the past decade, changed from being 'unusual' to becoming nationally institutionalised, to the point where it has become the focus of a major Parliamentary Inquiry which released its report 'Cancer of the bush or salvation for our cities' in early 2013 (Australian Government House of Representatives, 2013). It took over 232 submissions and 23 supplementary submissions. The Inquiry noted that specific and accurate data about the numbers of FiFo-related workers was very difficult to quantify, but it did note that a study in Western Australia in 2005 had identified nearly 47 percent of all mining workers were FiFo, and contractors to the mining industry had over 78 percent of their staff working as FiFo. The actual mode of working is in shifts, in some cases as long as six weeks on and one week off.

A large proportion of the Inquiry focused on medical practitioners, which it was clear referred to doctors, not nurses or human service workers. The title already suggests the paradox that this transition to new forms of working presents. Is this approach positive for those communities where such work is undertaken? Or negative because the workers themselves do not live in these communities? It would be fair to comment that while the Inquiry posed this question, it found no solution, and indeed, one of its members chose to offer a dissenting report.

The paradox at the heart of a FiFo approach is that while it may deliver some efficiencies in relation to workforce access, it does not foster local community development or allow for holistic practice. Where professionals travel from distant centres, they often do so to address the most serious problems – which tends to emphasise crisis management, rather than planning and prevention.

It needs stating here that FiFo is not just for one day – although it can be. If it is a component of employment contracts, it is more likely to be several days at a stretch, a week, two weeks, or even a month. The point about this form of practice is that the practitioner is not 'in place': there is always the sense of being 'out of place' that is – neither here nor there. As a powerful reminder of this fact, accommodation is provided for these workers. In the case of mining settlements, they may be cabins that are allocated as part of the work arrangements. In the case of human service workers, they are more likely to be within compounds in remote communities.

Our research tracked this adaptive change to practice, and we interviewed a number of professionals working as FiFo and living on-site within compounds. We concluded that this 'new' practice has had a direct change on roles: for example, juggling relationships (personal and professional); boundaries of professionalism; maintaining confidentiality; and role-specific tensions. The full detail of our findings can be found in the publications we have listed in our bibliography.

To set the scene, let's hear from Kay (a health practitioner) as she describes her work in a remote Queensland community:

> It remains my personal choice to choose this way of working. My life is a suitcase, laptop and a room … and any travel home to my family [860 kms away] is self-funded and on my days off.

Kay's experience is now of nearly 25 years of flying in/flying out of the Cape York area of far northern Queensland. The Cape

York community (1,300 people, primarily Aboriginal and Torres Strait Islander Australians) where Kay works is a flight of some two hours from Cairns (her hometown). It is possible to drive to the nearest of these communities (some twelve hours) but only in the dry season (May – October). In the monsoon season (the wet), roads are impassable, and all communities are effectively cut off except by air or sea. The Cape York region consists of more than 10 Aboriginal and Torres Strait Islander communities – some are designated as 'dry' and bringing alcohol into these communities is against the law. One large settlement – Weipa, and the nearby Aboriginal community of Napranum, is where bauxite is mined, but the majority of the Cape is wilderness and relies on tourism and the service sector for its economic base. Its major regional centre is Cooktown.

When she is working, Kay has a shift of four days on and three days off. During her time 'on,' her days can be up to 16 hours. While her clinic closes at 5:30 p.m., she usually spends her evenings on-site 'struggling with data entry.' Kay's work has become inextricably tied up with 'place'; as her duties become shaped by the way in which she lives temporarily and how she travels to and from her workplace. Working 'at a distance' from home demands a high degree of flexibility on her part. The workplace does not change to accommodate her – she has to change to accommodate it. In Kay's case, she lives on-site with other health professionals. 'We live in a compound. It has a fence around it. There is safety inside. After dark, I don't go outside. We have security guards.'

Another health professional we interviewed was Pat, with ten years of experience working in a large regional centre in Central

Queensland - the hub of a major coal mining area. Pat lives in the southeast of the state, and her travel time to her work community would also be 12 hours by road (she rarely does this) or a flight of just over an hour from the capital city, Brisbane. Pat lives north of Brisbane and also has a 32 km drive to the airport before she flies out.

Unlike Kay, Pat is a 'voluntary' FiFo – in other words, by contract, she is considered a 'local employee,' and while she does get some accommodation support, she receives no subsidies or support for her travel home, so she pays her own airfares to see her family, and she does so in her own time. For Pat, while her '… employer provided … accommodation [I] never knew who I would expect to wake up to in the next room … we had a shared bathroom and living areas,' she has now found her own accommodation.

Working remotely means that integration into the community demands a skilled, diplomatic approach. Pat found that '… many locals did not want to associate with FiFo employees [so] I would always identify myself as a local to protect myself from harmful comments berating (sic) how FiFo workers had '… started to destroy the town …' or '…. of course you are not a local, so you wouldn't understand ….'

Kay had also experienced the challenge of working intimately alongside her clients on a regular basis. Despite having worked in her community for many years, with an established relationship of trust with her community, she found that her professional decision-making was, on occasion, challenged. 'I have had to take a screaming child to the airport with people very upset. Mother drunk. There were 1,400 people in that community, and not one was prepared to care for that child, so I had to advocate for the child and take the child to Cairns.'

Both practitioners stressed the value of continuity of care as critical to the well-being of their patients and their communities. Pat suggested that '... having a transient population of medical and nursing staff with varying skills made [practicing in the community very] difficult as a nurse/midwife and often made it very confusing for clients when treatment plans/care constantly changed.' Kay agreed that '... the personal approach works best. If you are upfront and honest with [clients], that's best. Continuity is important. Follow-up is important.' Kay was able to sustain this continuity because she had been working in this region for over 20 years. She understood the place and its people. She was well aware of the need for cultural sensitivity and to advocate for a community where professionals from other agencies '... know nothing about the way the community works.'

We have spent some time discussing FiFo here as it has become an option of choice in the struggle to provide equity and access in remote settlements. Despite the many concerns expressed to the 2013 Review, more than a decade later, the practice is now entrenched and has almost become 'the norm.' While it appears, on the surface, to be a solution to the tyranny of distance, it has some obvious and immediate implications for social work practice. These include: the need for alternative education curricula for a future workforce; the potential lack of interest in working remotely (despite the increases in salaries); the continued demands of fractured and fragmented FiFo workforce families, and the social implications of these.

7 Community as landscape and built environment

We have discussed at length that community should be understood as more than just the built environment or the geographic landscape. However, there are times when both of these aspects of community become important components of our practice and to the way in which we understand our ecological framework.

First, the landscape. Rural communities are likely to have been historically settled for landscape reasons: because of a river, for example, or because of access to necessary resources. In the case of one community that we visited some years ago, in far western Queensland, its historic settlement was because it was halfway between two major ports (in one direction, south, it was over 2,000 kms) where sheep were shorn, the wool baled up for transport or herded (by foot, this was well before trucks) and then slaughtered and loaded on boats for the Empire. This community was surrounded by the landscape that enabled this form of sheep farming – wide-open spaces, and (then) much-needed grass. When we visited for the first time, we immediately noticed that we drove over a grid that formed part of a fence surrounding the whole settlement (some many hectares). There were two such grids, one in and one out of town. We discussed these with the locals and found that they had been erected in the past to enable the sheep to roam, but not to roam in the town. In the present day, however, they were being used for a very different purpose, as many of the locals had been shearers or farmhands during their working lives and had retired in the town, where some had developed forms of dementia. The fence and the grids enabled the community to ensure their safety from roaming, and it gave the men a recognised framework for their daily lives. This experience, and the way in which the community had supported their elderly members, has never left us.

Second, the built environment. No one rural community is the same as the next one. That is a truism, but particularly in relation to its built environment. In Australia, the historical reasons for the growth of many rural communities were the promise of finding gold. When we now visit those communities, we are struck by the beauty and occasionally, magnificence of their buildings. Gold built these. While they may have started their lives as banks or stock and station agents' premises, they are now more likely to be coffee shops, bars, or small museums.

However, not all of rural Australia was built on the back of gold or sheep. In the case of many places in far western Queensland and in northern Western Australia, it was water that was the reason why the settlement started. Watering the horses and cattle as they were driven to markets was a crucial aspect of survival in these places. One such place, some 800 kms inland north of Perth and on the edge of the Western Desert, was settled in the late nineteenth century, partly to ensure water and partly to fossick for gold. The gold has long since disappeared, but the settlement continues, with a current population of just over 700 and now acts as a supply centre for the region. The built environment here is a long way from the high Victorian brick edifices of the southern goldfields. It is a dusty place with tin roofs and one main street. Over half of the town's population are Aboriginal people drawn from a number of language groups from the Western

Desert. The history of pastoral Western Australia is that of colonisation and re-settlement. Driving into this town from the south of the state is driving through red dirt, and the town's buildings are also covered with red dust as the area has a very low average rainfall. It is the built environment that confronts the visitor, however, as every public building in the main street has large metal security screens on all the windows. The health professionals in town lived in a compound – creating their community by keeping those not wanted out. The message received was that this was not a safe place. It certainly provoked some level of distrust. 'As this was over a decade ago, and I have not returned, things may be different now, but the memory of this built environment has stayed with me' (Daniela).

8 Conclusions

As Australia moves into the third decade of the twenty-first century, it is very timely to consider 'what place rural Australia holds in our future?' – a question which, even a generation ago, would have been unthinkable. In seeking an answer, we can ask another, guided by C. Wright Mills: How could it be otherwise? Let's take our response from Kemmis (1990), by challenging the '… general placelessness of … political thought [that] weakens both our sense of politics and of place' by reclaiming a public life, through our agency, that understands and then practices '… its connection to a real, identifiable' place (as cited in Ardoin 2006, p. 117).

It may be a personal experience that your time in a rural community is very short. While it may be a work assignment, it could be to replace someone, and your time in this place is therefore limited. How does what we have described as understanding place and place attachment work when we are in place only briefly? Does someone in your office have that information? Is it possible to read material previously gathered? Yes, the internet can help here. There may be a connection through your networks to someone who has lived there previously or perhaps is still living there. Ask them to help. You will arrive in place with some context, and you will feel much less 'strange' as a result.

When you are there, take some time to talk to the local workers or people that you meet about what it is like to live there. You can explain that you want to know because you aren't there for long, but it is important to understand the place you are working in. People will respect your curiosity, and most will be happy to help you.

For those social workers who act as first responders to disasters such as floods or bushfires, having prior knowledge of the community is vital as they arrive to provide assistance in a time of trauma. We explore this further in the next chapter.

This chapter offers an alternative approach to rural practice, one which centres on an ecological (holistic, interactive, and adaptive) perspective resting on a place-based and strengths-based foundation, which is enabled through praxis – that is, testing our theory from practice evidence.

For the rural practitioner, working in a small community in an increasingly challenging landscape, both physically and emotionally, and aspiring to an alternative future for that place may appear a lonely, rather dispiriting task. (Re)valuing rural Australia is likely to come at a cost unless, as this chapter argues, by working alongside other like-minded individuals and building the alliances essential to enable this, by drawing on the strengths of others. These alliances need to be both broad and deep. They can and should be across disciplines, across professions, and within environments that may have not previously been considered as being 'useful' – they can be virtual or local, global, or intimate.

To succeed, they must absolutely be centred in place and within an ecological framework; one that values the strengths of that place and draws on it to enable a flourishing future. By building on our praxis experience and taking from the knowledge we have derived from that experience, we can aim to change our priorities. We can take our personal agency and share it with others – we can share our knowledge of, and love for, place. Sharing the narratives of successes and of challenges enables an honouring of both place and community, and in doing so, builds the capacity of everyone involved.

In our next chapter, we turn to the resources that we suggest can be valuable for rural practice.

Reflections from your experience

Think about a place where you feel you belong. How would you describe this place to someone you have just met? What are the aspects of this: landscape, memories, people? Or something else?

5
Community-focused strengths-based practice

Learning objectives

- Analyse the strengths and challenges in rural practice as they relate to the practitioner and the place
- Describe current approaches to strengths-based community work and how they might be applied
- Identify some new developments in policy, theory and practice and evaluate their potential for rural social work
- Articulate the key features of communities of practice and professional supervision and evaluate their effectiveness in rural practice settings

1 Introduction

To this point, we have explored the nature of rural communities in Australia and social workers' roles in supporting individuals, families, and communities. We have shared our own experiences as researchers and practitioners over several decades, as well as reflections from many generous rurally based practitioners, both established locals and newcomers. In addition, the people who live in these communities have shared their own stories of struggle, belonging, and strength, illustrating the power that a sense of place has in determining identity and shaping their lived experiences.

In this chapter, we bring together community-focused practice within a strengths-based ecological framework as a powerful approach for working in rural and remote communities. First, we explore the strengths and challenges of community-focused practice and propose how a strengths-based ecological approach might be applied in this work. We outline some of the qualities needed by practitioners in this work – for example, the knowledge, skills, and values, as well as how the concept of 'use-of-self', so central to reflective practice, applies specifically in this work.

Second, we also look to some of the current and future developments impacting rural social work. For example, we explain how recent social policy directions and associated practice approaches, such as the increasing investment in 'place-based' social policy and programs; the rapidly expanding IT technologies that enable communication, diagnostics, and counseling; and finally, increased accessibility to services by air for FiFo (fly in - fly out) and DiDo (drive in - drive out) models influence present-day practice.

Social work, as a discipline, has responded to new fields and challenges, some of which can be directly applicable to rural social work. These developments have contributed new knowledge to both theory and practice. The examples we present include environmental or 'green' social work, social work response to disasters, and newer models of community-led practice such as collective impact. These foster the identification of problems and development of local solutions wholly led by communities themselves, with little direct involvement of social work per se.

In our first chapter, we highlighted that working in rural communities is not a kind of utopia, nor can a single practitioner create the perfect or ideal community. Rather, we work with our own practice knowledge and skills, drawing on the strengths of the community to achieve better outcomes for everyone. It's primarily not about achieving concrete outcomes necessarily, as much as building relationships and working together.

2 Strengths and challenges

In our previous chapters, we have provided information, insights, and knowledge about rural communities and about rural practice, especially in Australia. Such work is both rewarding and challenging. We now further explore these various strengths and challenges. In keeping with our theme of listening to real voices and lived experiences, we have summarised these from the perspective of both the practitioner and of place. These are all drawn from our discussions with rural social workers and people in rural communities and can be described as: practitioner qualities that are all about you and practice qualities that are all about place. This is very much a shared approach.

2.1 All about you

From the outset, having respect for community and for Indigenous knowledge and people is critical. There is an opportunity for creativity in this work. Being a good communicator, being open and liking people, and being able to resolve conflicts and to offer yourself as a mediator are crucially valuable assets. These are traits that can be learned; they are not inherent. We can learn them on the job, from others, or we can bring them with us from our earlier experience and education. Reflecting on our conversations with rural practitioners, it has become apparent that many are self-reliant, flexible, and innovative in finding solutions for their clients and communities. They also tell us that they have developed these skills over time; sometimes out of necessity and sometimes by learning from others.

2.2 All about place

Place is fundamental to community-focussed practice. Drawing on the strengths of place enables the practitioner to build capacity and establish partnerships and alliances that all contribute to a flourishing community. Place gives us the framework within which we can address the complexity so inherent in rural social work. By sharing a common vision for place, the practitioner works alongside her community, contributing skills, knowledge, and competencies while at the same time valuing and learning from others.

On reflection, it soon becomes apparent that many of these qualities involve both challenge and opportunity. Social workers will be very familiar with such ambiguity given the nature of the ever-present ethical and moral dilemmas and multiple perspectives from which to determine how to proceed. Judgment and critical reflection are central to all social work practice, but perhaps even more so in rural work.

Qualities of being innovative or creative, liking people, or being of upstanding character are not obviously included in the social work curriculum, whereas communication, community development, Indigenous knowledge, and others are topics that are covered. Within this list, a theme of 'going above and beyond', or going the 'extra yard' emerges. Being ultra-resilient or a master of all trades, self-reliance all suggest this extra level of ability and motivation. The cluster of qualities relating to practice are more customary and indicate predictable areas of knowledge, theory, and skills. These include being collaborative, developing partnerships, dealing with complexity, and perhaps most crucially, finding a suitable practice framework. We will return to the topic later in Chapter 6.

2.3 The problem of churn

In Chapter 2, we introduced the notion of 'churn'. This refers to the difficulties with recruitment and retention of staff in many rural and remote communities, which leads to a succession of new staff often interspersed with periods of positions remaining unfilled for months or even years in some cases. Over time, this can lead to a level of distrust of any new arrival in the community. We have heard many comments about new arrivals from locals in these communities such as 'Well, they won't last' or 'Why bother? They will be gone next week.' In these situations, a new social worker has an added task to overcome distrust and engage with a community that harbors a reluctance to do so. This is not an issue only for social work. High turnover and consequent churn affect many sectors – education, law enforcement, industry, and others – and is escalating, especially among health professionals:

Rural Queensland is losing healthcare workers at a frightening rate — five per cent higher than in metro areas — sparking a dire warning from the peak medical body (Simmerton, 2025)

2.4 Personal and professional isolation

Isolation, geographically, professionally, and personally, are well-documented experiences reported by practitioners working in rural and remote communities. As well as the long distance from major centres and the lack of access to many resources, the reality of working as a sole social worker can pose challenges for a newly arrived practitioner. It is useful here to consider personal and professional isolation separately. Lack of community connection is a common form of personal isolation. In cities, people will have connections through networks of family, friends, at the gym, places, and spaces they have, in fact, chosen and are familiar with. One can simply choose to be involved or not. However, in rural communities, this is less likely to be the case. Our colleague from rural Canada, Flo Frank, explains:

> Disconnection in rural communities is way less likely. Most small places have a tradition of 'coffee row'. You know a gathering place mostly where older people, and other locals come to chat and have morning coffee. It's always public and usually the coffee is terrible but it's where you find out the price of corn, who's got a new tractor, who's sick and whose aunt is visiting (Frank 2025, pers. com).

In outback Australia now, these places look a bit different – the local pub, the post office agent, in a fancier café, or outside a visiting medical clinic. The coffee may be better, but the connections, the information shared, and the opinions expressed remain important. Starting out, it is these spaces and places that are key for the worker to make early contact with, as it is here that initial connections can be made, potential groups to join shared, and important information about the community can be gleaned.

Professional isolation involves another set of issues, however. Supervision is regarded as a central tenet of social work practice. Historically, it has been the process by which practitioners can reflect on their practice, talk through ethical dilemmas, obtain professional development, and develop new skills. For many social workers, access to supervision is a key factor in remaining in difficult roles, so it's crucial in addressing workforce retention.

There has been growing concern that access to professional supervision is declining (Howard, Katrak, Blakemore & Pallas, 2016). There is a distinct difference between managerial supervision for administrative tasks and professional supervision to enhance and ensure professional practice. In rural and remote communities, having access to independent professional supervision is increasingly difficult. In their comprehensive study of rural, regional, and remote social work in Australia, Howard et al. (2016) found the majority of practitioners had either no or very poor professional supervision. For some, supervision was obtained only from their line manager as part of organisational support, but the focus was much more on administrative tasks.

This situation has fostered creative and innovative responses in many rural and remote settings. Rural social workers have sought out peer supervision or support from colleagues and other networks to overcome these gaps. Howard et al (2016) describe the tenacity with which social workers made these connections despite challenging environments and often little support from their employing organisation.

The availability of online communication has offered new ways to engage with supervisors and provides a space to undertake that all-important critical reflection and professional development. This is another example of private-for-profit practitioners filling a gap. This is an issue to follow into the future as it remains to be seen whether such resources can actually increase the numbers of professional supervisors available in rural areas and the overall quality of social work services.

2.5 'Belonging' to the community

To be effective, the rural practitioner has to 'belong' to the community in which they work. If we are to draw upon community strengths, resources, and capacities, it is crucial that we become involved within that community at many levels beyond the professional. This can entail going beyond specific job descriptions, to work across borders and boundaries to adopt a holistic community focus. This may extend to broader areas of social planning, service coordination, community development, and networking, often with far more effort required than one's urban counterparts. It can involve such diverse activities as joining a local sporting team (building networks) to participating in a community meeting raising concerns about the closure of a local industry. This may ensue a subtle shift in identity – from the urban to the rural. Furthermore, the dilemma of managing dual or multiple relationships, as discussed in Chapter 2, is a regular occurrence. Rural practitioners will need to ensure that boundaries in relationships are very clear.

2.6 On stigma and stereotyping

In Chapter 1, we described how stereotyping 'the rural' has become a deeply-seated aspect of Australian society. In fact, it is so deeply ingrained that most of us are not aware of it. In the process of stereotyping, we create stigma on those we stereotype. For the rural social work practitioner, it may come as a shock to realise that they are also stigmatised when they undertake their practice. Why? It is a shock because it may be the first time that they, personally, have experienced such stigma. It can also come as a shock to realise that their clients, people that they serve through their practice, are stigmatised by the wider society, and that by working alongside them, they are too.

Stigma, as Erving Goffman (1963) wrote over six decades ago, is experienced by the individual as patronisation, humiliation, discomfort, or devaluation. We speak of the 'back of beyond' as living in remote Australia: those who live there are less important than those who live here – at the centre, where it all happens. Stigmatisation happens across society, across groups. When Daniela first joined a regional university (over 600 km north of the capital city), she discovered that

> Working within regional universities, sociologists often hear colleagues and students speak about the regional/rural – often disparagingly, frequently with despair – as though 'nothing happens ', 'everything is happening somewhere else'. Some colleagues still see the regional

university as a waiting room – waiting to move to an urban university, a 'real place' (Stehlik, 2001, p. 32).

The stereotyping of a regional university transitions to the stereotyping of those who work there, and they, in turn, feel that devaluation as stigma. It then also affects the students. In a broader sense, this self-awareness comes to all of us who have experienced stigmatisation. It will also come to our social worker when they realise that they have been cast into the same descriptor as their clients.

In Chapter 3 we wrote about the stigmatising experience many felt as they sought government assistance during the Millennium drought. This was a direct result of them previously stereotyping such individuals as 'dole bludgers' or 'welfare cheats'. Now they were in that group, an experience that was both confronting and life-changing for them. They also found themselves being ostracised by others in their communities as seeking help was very hard indeed for those who prided themselves on being stoic.

In Chapter 4, we introduced Pat, who worked away from home, in a mining community distant from her family. However, Pat understood the delicate balance between being a FiFo and being a 'local'. She avoided the stigma of FiFo by identifying herself as a local, as she had actually worked in this town for some years. She had experienced stigma verbally, through the language in which her clients spoke of the 'other'. She was made acutely aware that it was FiFo workers who had 'started to destroy the town' or, more commonly, being told, 'you are not a local so you wouldn't understand'.

Let's look at this example of stigmatisation more closely. From the point of view of the 'local' residents, they experienced the distancing and separation associated with living in a place that was not appealing enough to settle in more permanently. They understood that this was because their town was less than desirable, as it was hot, inland, away from the coast, with apparently little of interest to recommend it. The local residents interpreted that this meant that they too were of little interest, choosing, as they did, to live in this apparently undesirable place. From Pat's point of view, having worked in this town for some years, she understood this sense of detachment from other places as a strategy to cope with the stigmatisation she experienced. To enable her to work more practically and with less distance with her clients, she chose to call herself a local. Pat understood that this would enable her to deal with any of the barriers raised, and it would strengthen her ability to provide what her clients needed, which was a creative solution.

How then can our social work practitioner deal with the stigma that will inevitably become part of daily life in their rural or remote community? First, and importantly, they will need to foster her self-awareness and the language with which to talk about and communicate with clients and the community. The alliances, networks, and partnerships they establish will support her in this strategy. Speaking positively of place, its history, its culture, and its people will strengthen their resolve. By drawing on local knowledge (strengths), they will be able to tap into what Tomaney (2013) calls the 'virtue of parochialism' with its attachment to place and its recognition of place identity. Tomaney goes on to suggest that '... the local, its cultures and its solidarities are a moral starting point and a locus of ecological concern in all societies and at all moments in history'; a point which links

him to Cuomo's ecological flourishing (https://doi.org/10.1177/
0309132512471235 Accessed: 11th January 2025) as we introduced it in the previous chapter.

So, how to respond to these challenges?

3 Strengths-based practice approaches in community work

Strengths-based practice (SBP) is well established in social work
(Saleebey, 2013). Originally developed in the mental health field
in the social work school at the University of Kansas, it has found
application in many fields of practice, including making the transition to community practice in rural communities. Strengths-
based practice has its critics because its focus on strengths can
mean that crucial needs are missed or overlooked.

Strengths approaches work within critical life domains - individual, family, work, education, and community connections.
Daley & Avant (2013) argue that issues relating to rural people
in terms of individuals, families, groups, and other systems are
actually intertwined with the whole community environment.
They propose a multi-systems perspective to rural practice. Their
model employs strength perspective approaches to identify
community assets and existing coping skills of people while still
maintaining a problem-solving approach. The difference here is
that more traditional social work approaches, especially in rural
communities, tend to focus on the deficits: what services are
missing, what skills are missing, rather than seeking out what
assets the community might hold. We see examples of this kind
of approach in some of the work in responding to disasters in

rural communities. In Australia, natural disasters such as bush-fires and droughts impact rural communities more severely than cities. Writing on experiences of the 2013 bushfires in rural New South Wales

> Our philosophy was that people are all capable and resil-ient and able to make their own decisions . . . and (being) on the lookout for where strength-based conversations come in . . . It was astounding seeing people's resil-ience and strength, and I found so many of them just incredibly inspiring, and just seeing the love really that exists, and the hope that exists (in Rich, Booth, Reddy & Rowlands 2014: 34–35).

Earlier in chapter 4 we explored the notion of flourishing as an ethic in working in rural communities and posed the question as to whether a practitioner can work towards community flourish-ing as a strategy beyond resilience. It is here that strength-based approaches, working within ecological frameworks, can offer a model for achieving this. It would be advisable, therefore, for the potential rural practitioner to gain some experience or aware-ness of these approaches.

However, strengths-based community practice needs also to be culturally compatible with rural life. That means gaining an appreciation and knowledge of rural life and people. Social workers must have a holistic view, knowledge that spans geog-raphy, economics, sociology, politics, and policy (Green, 2003). It is important to utilise knowledge gained from the community and its members and to work in ways sensitive to the commu-nity. Practitioners need to be flexible, creative, and able to impro-vise to provide services in locally relevant ways (Cheers, 1998;

Martinez-Brawley, 2000). Working in collaboration with others offers opportunities to enable culturally sensitive practice. If we accept that all community members have skills to contribute, we not only involve them, but also ensure that we are 'not alone' in this endeavor. Drawing on her own extensive experience, Flo Frank encourages us to consider the young people in the community as having an opportunity to contribute. She writes:

> Community development provides a powerful process for the support and development of young people and those who are marginalised. For example, some young people may have the skills, but little work experience (Frank & Smith 2006, p. 55).

By actively involving young people in our strengths-based practice approach, we are providing them with experience while drawing on their skills. We are also, importantly, setting a foundation for their future contributions to their community.

We have touched on a number of aspects of SBA as it applies to working within rural communities. While we appreciate that there are challenges in working in this way, we argue that this integration offers a promising alternative to current approaches.

4 Looking to the future

While at its core, rural social work practice has remained the same, other developments have had an impact on social work and social workers. We cover some of these here but encourage you to follow up on developments in technologies, changes in policy agendas, and newer service delivery models. The following are four examples of opportunities that may encourage you to integrate into your rural practice.

4.1 Place based policies and programs

In recent years we have seen an emerging 'place-based' social policy agenda. Place-based approaches are defined as

> … collaborative endeavours that seek to create systemic change by bringing together efforts across the community to work towards shared long-term outcomes. Place-based approaches have been used to address community need by harnessing the vision, resources and opportunities of community (Queensland Council of Social Service [QCOSS], 2019, https://www.qcoss.org.au/ Accessed 12th Feb 2025).

These programs have been seen as a potential response to communities with 'complex needs' that consume considerable government resources and expenditure. Place-based approaches have two main aims – first, to address those complex needs and problems more effectively, and second, to build strong, cohesive communities. These have been recognised globally as effective in responding to disasters, pandemics, health issues, or education, and more significantly in situations where traditional service delivery has not worked. Key elements include strong partnerships that foster collaboration, governance that is community-led, including all levels of government, service providers, businesses, community groups, as well as citizens.

A recent example in Australia is the national Stronger People, Stronger Places initiative established by the Federal government as a 'community-led, partnership initiative designed to improve the lives of children and their families' (Australian Government, Department of Social Services, 2025). It is important to note here that of the ten communities involved, four are located in rural areas, three are in remote areas, and three are in regional centres. None are in capital cities. The focus of this Scheme is on place. The selection of sites highlighted higher levels of disadvantage and need outside the capital cities.

As social workers, we need to be mindful to apply a critical lens to the context of our practice and how we respond. In the era of neo-liberal policies and programs, the question becomes to what extent will place-based approaches be used by governments as a means to divest themselves of responsibility to address areas of high need? We discussed the impact of neo-liberalism, individual responsibility, competitive tendering, technocratic interventions, etc., on community development in Chapter 3. This has been starkly revealed since 2015 with the introduction of the National Disability Insurance Scheme (NDIS) in Australia. All disability funding is now linked to an individual across all states and territories. There are few options for funds to develop any community capacity to welcome and include people with disabilities, a crucial aspect of promoting a flourishing life in the community. The Scheme's introduction has been highly problematic, creating extensive funding overspends and requiring several major reviews.

Shaw (2008) argued that the notion of 'community' has been 'appropriated' to justify a wide range of political positions, known as the 'politics of community' (cited in Lynch et al., 2020, p. 248). However, it is important to stress that in its continued pursuit of social justice, social work has utilised the politics of community as a means to investigate social inequalities in advocacy and activism.

We argue that place-based initiatives can be useful opportunities for rural social workers. They can provide support for community mobilising, bring additional funding, not for service provision, but for whole community initiatives, foster and support community leaders, and bring previously isolated and separate sectors together in collaboration.

Logan Together is a Collective Impact project in South East Queensland that has made progress in improving outcomes for children in a specific place but perhaps more importantly, has built a community-led movement. Collective Impact, in general terms, has five key conditions: a common agenda; continuous communication; mutually reinforcing activities; backbone support; and shared measurement. Logan Together began as an idea for starting to address the gap in health, education, and social Outcomes for its children aged zero to eight. Some 14 years later, it is continuing and growing.

> I was privileged to be involved in this movement from the outset. Working in a community with multiple disadvantages where too many kids were left behind, on too many fronts – health, education and social outcomes and national child development indicators. Governments had poured hundreds of millions of dollars into services over many years – with little or no change for kids and their families. Starting with shared concerns by many community members, government officials and service providers, the idea of Logan Together was formed and grew. It has steadfastly held on to the principle that the only way positive change can happen for kids is to listen to the community and work together with that community. Its three pillars are First Nations first, Children at the heart, and Community led. (Lesley).

These examples show how place-based approaches have gained some momentum and achieved some positive outcomes for communities. Time will tell whether this is a policy 'fad' or whether it can become an integral part of supporting rural communities.

4.2 Environmental or green social work (GSW)

In recent years, environmental social work has emerged as a new but legitimate field of practice. A strong case has been made for GSW in the literature, but its practical application has been limited (Ramsay & Boddy, 2017). Certainly, changing natural environments, impacts on agriculture, and climate-caused disasters are increasingly pressing issues for rural communities, and rural social workers have been on the ground responding to these. Green social work (GSW) or environmental social work (ESW) is a form of social work practice that:

> … focuses on how the social organisation of relationships between peoples and their interaction with the flora and fauna in their physical habitats create [today's] socio-economic and physical environmental crises that undermine the well-being of human beings and planet earth (Dominelli, 2012, p. 25).

Green social work structures draw on well-established frameworks such as ecological social work, international social work, eco-feminist social work, and anti-oppressive practice (Ramsay & Boddy, 2017). These offer potential additional resources for the rural practitioner to inform and guide their practice. To date, there has been little attention given to green social work in social work training and education, and a relative absence of social work voices from the broader environmental discourse.

However, there is potential here for further work in theory and practice to highlight the contributions of social work to rural communities, especially in our understandings of intersectionality – how people are treated based on their multiple identities of disadvantage, for example, gender, ethnicity, and rurality. Social justice easily translates into environmental justice, and social work is well acquainted with how power inequalities interact with and influence social relationships. It is prudent, therefore, for rural social work to keep abreast of these developments that can and are impacting their work.

5 Strategies for strengths-based community practice

Social workers draw upon many resources and strategies to support their practice. However, we offer two specific strategies that may support strengths-based community practice in rural communities. These are, first, to take advantage of professional supervision and other continuing education opportunities, and second, to seek a community of practice or similar inter-agency group or network.

5.1 Professional development and practice supervision

As we look to the future, the provision of professional supervision remains a crucial and long-standing tradition in social work. Many professional codes of ethics require practitioners to have regular professional supervision. Students' first experience of supervision is usually during their practicum, being guided by an experienced social worker.

As we have discussed in various chapters, this can be difficult to access in rural and remote postings where there may be few suitably qualified staff and prohibitive distances between the worker and supervisors. The availability of professional social work supervision has declined significantly, especially in rural settings. Many practitioners, therefore, devise creative ways to gain support personally and professionally. Some suggestions and comments we have gathered and discussed in previous chapters include developing good networks and partnerships with other agencies, making the most of peer supervision and collegial support, as well as looking out for relevant online training and workshops. Keeping a list of contacts who can be just a phone call away is a good interim measure.

5.2 Communities of practice

Communities of practice were introduced in Chapter 3. Here we further develop these as potential tools for future practice. You will recall that in her experiences working in rural communities, Cheryl talked about how important it was to develop relationships and gather a support group around her. In more recent years, we have come to see the value of what is now known as a community of practice. A community of practice is a group of people who share a common concern or common interest in a topic and who come together to share ideas, develop best practices, and create new knowledge. While this has originally been in the form of face-to-face meetings, more recently these have become known as virtual communities of practice. Becoming involved or a member of a community practice is a really valuable strategy for rural social workers, particularly those who are working in isolated areas with little opportunity for contact with fellow practitioners.

It's interesting to note that the earliest virtual communities of practice were developed in rural areas. These were pioneered in Alberta, Canada, as well as other isolated communities. The technologies for these were further enhanced in response to the global COVID-19 pandemic, where many practitioners were working in isolation with little opportunity to engage with others.

When first starting out in a rural community, it's certainly worthwhile seeking out others with shared experiences and goals. You may find you have to initiate a community of practice if one is not already established. The initial step, therefore, may be meeting others in the community who share the vision for that community and/or are addressing similar problems. Previously, many communities had an interagency group made up of employees of various government agencies such as child protection, social security, non-government community agencies (NGOs), and perhaps police and local government. These met regularly as a way to coordinate services, share knowledge, and address problems. These may still function in some communities and can be a useful support for the rural social worker.

Communities of Practice are a more recent development and will likely include people living outside the community rather than people one works with every day. As mentioned previously, the availability of online meeting technology has greatly expanded the possibilities. Features of a CoP include having shared concerns and a desire to address them, a willingness to share ideas and resources, and a commitment to regular meetings. CoPs are therefore more formal and usually led by a facilitator to keep track of progress. Regular review of how the CoP is working is also a key feature, as is a willingness to make changes if things aren't working.

6 Conclusions

This chapter has focused squarely on practice in rural communities. Initially canvassing some of the strengths and challenges of community practice, it explored some of the valued qualities of practitioners seeking to enter this field. Some of the recent developments in policies and practice approaches were also discussed. Newer fields such as environmental or green social work were introduced. Several strategies to support community-focused strengths-based practice were presented, including participating in a community of practice and seeking innovative ways to obtain professional supervision and support.

In the following and final chapter, we focus on practical guidance and resources to support your rural practice journey. We present these along a timeline of preparing, entering, and working in your rural community.

Reflections from your experience

What are some of the strengths and challenges that a new graduate might experience in taking up a rural post? How could some of these be addressed?

Find some examples of place-based programs or projects. What are the key features of these—e.g., what are they trying to address? What is the broad approach used? Where is the program located?

Could the program be adapted or applied in a remote community? How could this be implemented? What potential difficulties might be encountered?

6
Ready, set, go – your rural practice journey

Learning objectives

- Outline the steps in taking up a role working in a social work role in rural communities.
- Develop and Reflect on a preliminary practice framework for rural social work and outline its key characteristics.
- Articulate some of the current issues facing rural communities in Australia today.

1 Introduction

This final chapter is about the 'doing' of rural social work. It brings together what has been covered in previous chapters and translates it into practice. The goal here is to offer practical guidance to the beginning rural social worker. We have used the metaphor of a journey, travelling along a timeline through different terrain, perhaps taking a side road or two, and gathering companions along the way. The 'journey' idea is not new. Lesley, with her colleague Donna, used this in their introductory social work text now in its seventh edition (Chenoweth & McAuliffe, 2021).

Students for almost 20 years have found this metaphor to be helpful, and we have not found a better one as yet. The chapter now identifies the seven steps in this journey, which are discussed further below.

Our journey begins with getting ready, i.e., the preparation for practice during social work studies and field experiences. It then moves to preparing to start your rural social work position, your role, exploring the place and the community in which you will live and work. How do you enter this community? Once you are established and underway, we present some guidance about working alongside Aboriginal and Torres Strait Islander peoples living in the community and how to gather support through networks both personally and professionally. Finally, we offer some pointers on how to leave and move on once your period of employment is completed.

In the concluding section, we return to resilience and flourishing. We reflect on the current situation in rural Australia through a selection of recent articles depicting the gamut of rural and remote communities: the difficulties, the extreme challenges of climate and economic turbulence, the signs of new developments, and newer residents and the contributions of travellers who are here for a shorter period of time.

1.1 Getting ready

Having specific coverage of rural practice in the social work curriculum is certainly an advantage. This can include material about rural sociology, social policy analysis with a focus on rural issues, and skill development in group work and community practice. In our experience, this varies across different degree programs.

Not surprisingly, Australian universities that are rurally based or connected tend to offer more options for community and rural practice learning experiences. Some programs offer choices in electives across other disciplines such as rural sociology, rural studies, or community development. If you have similar options and are considering working in rural communities, then it would be advantageous to include these in your degree. For other workers who did not have such options, seeking out professional development opportunities for workshops, seminars, or additional courses that provide this content could be useful.

1.2 Field placements

Field placements are core to social work education, offering opportunities to experience work in different fields of practice within various organisational settings and with a variety of client groups. More importantly, they provide an opportunity to have regular personalised professional supervision in integrating one's knowledge and skills through reflective practice. Opportunities to undertake placements in rural communities are somewhat difficult, particularly for students in city-based universities. Universities located in regional or rural centres are more likely to offer placement opportunities, though these are fewer in number.

In our work, we found that undertaking a rural placement was often prohibitive financially and logistically. Making such opportunities available will require investment and planning. A recent national program in Australia charged with increasing opportunities for students to undertake placements in mental health settings included a targeted approach to incremental health placement in rural settings. This included funding for students to cover some of their expenses and for agencies to support them in taking students. This program has led to some promising signs, as students with no experience in rural settings were very positive about their rural social work placements. Students spoke about learning so much in their rural pracs, both professionally and personally, and expressed a hope that more students would take up the opportunity.

National Mental Health Pathways to Practice Program Pilot, 2023–24, and cited in

(https://www.health.gov.au/sites/national-mental-health-workforce-strategy-2022-2032 (National Mental Health Pathways to Practice, 2025) Accessed February 2025.)

If you have an opportunity, taking a rural placement is an excellent way to gain some exposure and experience. However, there is a need for future investment in targeted programs to support more placements if we are to recruit and prepare more rural social workers.

1.3 Preparing to start your rural job

Before taking up your rural employment, there are several aspects to consider in planning and preparing. These include doing research on the community and the areas in which you will work, especially if this place is new to you. Questions to guide you can include: What are the main features of the location, its geography, its history, and demographics? Who lives there? What are the main industries or sources of employment? What community resources and facilities are there locally or nearby?

You will also need to take account of the different kinds of roles and the organisations that employ social workers. For example, many rural and remote roles are within Federal and state government agencies such as child protection, youth justice, or health services. These are usually statutory roles – that is, they have provisions under legislation, are usually enacted by government employees, and have outcomes directly linked to the objectives of the legislation. The most common and familiar example of statutory work is policing. Officers are charged with enforcing laws, maintaining public order, investigating incidents or offences, and have statutory powers to do this. Statutory social work roles have responsibilities and expectations set out in relevant legislation. Child protection work is guided by legislation aimed at keeping children safe, and parole officers have responsibilities under corrections and judicial orders. Statutory roles are often viewed differently in rural communities. There may be people who mistrust a worker 'from the government,' but others see upholding laws and protecting the community as crucial and perhaps high-status jobs.

As we detailed earlier, social workers in roles other than those that are statutory are more likely to be employed by not-for-profits (NFPs) or non-government organisations (NGOs). These may be faith-based or other kinds of charities. If you are working with a non-government organisation (NGO), it is likely to be funded primarily through government grants. These can be annual or triennial, and the larger the NGO (that is, whether it is national, state-based, or local), the larger the grant. Managing the government's funding of your agency comes with an expectation that your organisation follows certain government guidelines and possibly undergoes regular auditing and evaluation of such expenditure. This will require you to maintain accurate records, as your NGO administration will advise.

In Chapter 1 we introduced the issue of social workers employed in for-profit businesses or being private providers of social work services, or perhaps even small business owners. The number of social workers in for-profit organisations or in private practice has increased over the past decade in Australia, including in regional centres and rural towns, especially with the introduction of the National Disability Insurance Scheme (NDIS). The latest figures identify nearly 25,000 national small businesses that are providers under the NDIS (Australian Government, National Disability Insurance Scheme, 2025 at https://dataresearch.ndis.gov.au (Accessed: 8th February, 2025).

1.4 Entering your community

We can enter a community in a variety of ways. We can be there for a short time, or we can be planning for a substantial career. The way in which we enter, the strategies we adopt, and the people who introduce us all make a difference in the long term. You may need to travel to this community prior to your formal start date. If you can, take up this opportunity. You will be introduced to a variety of people, some of whom have formal titles of leadership. There will be others who may appear less important. These may be people who are the holders of history and have an important influence on others. They are often the people who will tell you, 'this is how this community works.' We encourage you to listen to them.

Your organisation will operate within specific boundaries to your area of responsibility. In outback Australia, these are usually large, sometimes covering hundreds of kilometres between settlements. Gaining an appreciation of these distances and areas may take time, but it is advisable to understand as much as you can about the terrain and the borders. We have discussed the issue of borders previously, whereby there are often 'official' borders designated by a government department, for example. But the interpretation of the 'border' can be determined by local residents and often, too, by the practitioner who may extend their service to those in need beyond the official line.

Rural and remote areas in Australia are home to many Aboriginal and/or Torres Strait Islander people. We detailed in Chapter 1 that these groups constitute approximately 20 per cent of the population in remote communities and more than 47 per cent in very remote areas (AIHW, 2024). Therefore, social work in rural and remote communities always involves some level of engagement with and living and working alongside Aboriginal and Torres Strait Islander peoples. The context is similar in rural and remote communities in Canada (First Nations and Inuit), parts of the United States (First Nations), and Northern Europe (Sami peoples).

Social work with Aboriginal people in Australia is complex and becomes even more so for practitioners working in remote rural communities that are already disadvantaged. This requires a broad knowledge base that includes the history of Aboriginal peoples, the impact of colonisation over centuries through policies and practices, impacts that persist in the lived experiences of First Peoples today, and importantly, the role of social work in that history (Bennett, Zubrzycki & Bacon, 2011). For example, in Australia, the removal of children by authorities, known as the Stolen Generations, the alarmingly high rates of incarceration, and children in care against the context of extreme marginalisation in rural areas are common experiences contributing to intergenerational trauma. Social workers will find it helpful to draw upon the knowledge and theories of trauma, racism, Whiteness, human rights, and critical practice.

It is beyond the scope of this publication to explore these topics in full. As non-Indigenous practitioners, we are indebted to Aboriginal social work researchers, practitioners, and teachers who have made an enormous contribution to our knowledge, theory, and practice in this work.

Bennett, Zubrzycki, & Bacon (2011) propose a practice framework for social work with Aboriginal people and their communities. The framework includes the usual components of knowledge, skills, and values and emphasises the importance of having a deep awareness of one's own journey and identity – i.e., critical knowledge of oneself. Who is your family, where are you from, what are your personal values, and why do you want to work with Indigenous people? Knowledge beyond those areas mentioned earlier includes Indigenous spirituality and worldviews, the connections people have to country, the cultural protocols, the important stories, and who the Elders are – who do I ask? The framework highlights the importance of the values of respect and reciprocity, being humble, and being genuine. Skills include deep listening, silence, observing, self-disclosure, showing empathy, and reflection. The two central concepts across these components are relationships and cultural courage. Cultural courage refers to the 'destination of being with and not doing to' (Bennett et al, 2011, p. 34). It also means to understand one's own cultural background and privilege and how that impacts on how we relate to others and to acknowledge one's fears and anxieties.

Drawing on this body of work, we present a range of useful principles, resources, and knowledge for a new practitioner working in Aboriginal communities. The critical aspects of your practice approach when working alongside Aboriginal people include being respectful and taking the time to listen. This process of sitting down to listen and spending time with Aboriginal people is called 'yarning'. Through yarning, we can learn about the local community, culture, Aboriginal knowledge, and consult with Elders. Importantly, it is a way to begin the process of building relationships and working together, and it takes time.

There is increasing availability of resources and frameworks to support social work practice with Indigenous communities. For example, Jacob Prehn (2024) has developed an Indigenous strengths-based theoretical framework that identifies and prioritises the strengths within Aboriginal cultures to combat the dominant deficit narratives. His framework centres on an Indigenous worldview, inclusive of epistemology (knowledge), ontology (way of being), and axiology (values), and offers six core principles for use in practice. Stewart & Allan (2013) proposed a cultural mapping tool for establishing relationships with Indigenous people and Bennett and her colleagues have developed tools for continuous improvement in cultural responsiveness (see also Bennett & Morse, 2023).

1.5 Building your networks

In earlier chapters, we discussed the value of garnering supports and building alliances. This included seeking out potential partners through your workplace and other agencies and looking into other opportunities to connect with people socially.

Often, the best way to start this process is through ordinary places where people gather, for example, a coffee haunt or café, local football or cricket ground, or a general store. If you have family that has moved with you, you may make contacts through the school or a sports club.

It will soon become apparent that these relationships could create potential conflicts of interest. The nature of dual relationships, as we have previously discussed, is that some people you might encounter through your work role can also be people that you meet socially or share common interests.

The value of professional supervision and collegial support has been discussed in the previous chapter. At a fundamental practical level, professional supervision outside the work organisation is often very difficult to achieve. Rural social workers employ a whole range of innovative ways to build these connections. Finding out if there is an existing inter-agency committee or group that meets regularly is a helpful first step. This might be a formally constituted group, with regular meeting dates, through to more ad hoc arrangements, perhaps on an as-needed basis.

Searching for online opportunities is also a good strategy. These are usually available through your professional association, such as the Australian Association of Social Workers (AASW), which offers professional development courses or seminars.

1.6 Exiting

Closure in social work practice is always a key aspect of all interventions, be they individual, group, or with whole communities. In rural communities, the process of 'ending well' is important for both the community and for the social worker – perhaps more so than in city-based practice. Reasons for exiting a community-based position are many and varied. A worker may have another job offer with a promotion or need to move for personal reasons such as accessing schools for their children, or the isolation and rural life just isn't for them.

From the community's perspective, departures may be viewed as yet another failure of policy and services to deliver what rural communities need; and that most professionals don't want to work in these places (or with our community). The community may experience a sense of loss as yet another practitioner is leaving, with a long wait for another to replace them; that is, the 'churn' continues. It is therefore prudent to take additional time and give more thought to the leaving process, if at all possible.

Some of the established steps in closure or 'termination' in the social work practice literature certainly apply to rural communities. As always, a planned process is preferable, if possible, whereby the people in the community and colleagues have as much notice as possible. It is helpful to allow time for all parties to acknowledge and process any feelings. Reviewing what has been achieved and what needs to be continued or changed is also important. There may be an opportunity for final meetings or even a farewell gathering. At this point, it is salutary to recall our discussion in Chapter 1 that social work in rural communities is not necessarily about achieving measurable outcomes or some kind of utopia for the community. The relationships, collaborations, and partnerships that are facilitated by the practitioner with the community are often valued as a process in itself and can be helpful for the next person in the role.

1.7 Your practice framework

A practice framework provides a foundation for practice. It combines knowledge, values, and skills to guide your practice, to make it purposeful and relevant to the context in which you are working (Chenoweth & McAuliffe, 2021). Practice frameworks evolve over time and adapt to different situations, new knowledge, and skills. Students begin this process while still learning and continue to develop and change it over time. Essential features of a practice framework include being consistent with the purpose and ethics of the profession, based on empirical foundations, and providing guidance for the worker to work through complex situations. At the heart of all practice is the notion of use of self, that is, that you, the worker, are the key to practice through all the relationships within the work. Throughout this text, we have discussed how crucial relationships are to all aspects of rural social work. Developing or modifying your practice framework will be a key undertaking if you begin working in this domain. The student exercise below provides a starting point for developing a practice framework.

2 Conclusions

The next section summarises each of our chapters as we come to our conclusions. Chapter 1 explained how we gathered the various evidence and narratives we draw on here. It outlined the purpose of the book and set out some definitions we use. It gave an overview of Australia, its landscape, peoples, and history. It then described how human services and social work integrate with this history and place. Chapter 2 took up the issues of rurality and social work and how practice is different outside urban settings. We answer the question: who are the social workers in rural communities today? We discussed some of the unique issues associated with working rurally and how these amplify in our practice. Chapter 3 explored how the paradox of community, as both construction and reality, plays out in our practice. We gave examples from the lived experience of both practitioners and community members. We analysed just how vague 'community' is defined in both policy and social work standards. Chapter 4 integrated place and identity within a strengths-based ecological practice. This framework, we argue, can offer a positive and comprehensive approach to the challenges of working rurally. We argue for a re-integration of community development into the social work curriculum, too long neglected. Chapter 5 described the strengths and challenges of community-focused practice and proposed how a strengths-based ecological approach may be applied. We describe some interesting new developments in social work that can be useful in working rurally. In this final chapter, we offered seven steps in a journey to working in rural and remote communities.

3 What of the future? …

As we write this in early 2025, the future of rural Australia beyond 2025 is mixed. With a Federal election mid-year, there is much media attention on rural and remote communities, where previously there was silence. This is usual in our election cycles, though the volume appears louder this cycle. We have taken a number of these stories that illustrate current concerns and opportunities, and some that give you, the reader, a glimpse of how we live today. So here is a selective pastiche of life in the bush.

Our first story is one that is repeated regularly. It is about the lack of health services and the difficulty rural towns have in attracting medical practitioners. This item highlights the severe shortfall of medical General Practitioners (GPs), which disproportionately affects rural towns, leading to many communities 'offering huge salary packages … and in some cases, free housing' to attract doctors to move there.

'GP shortages sting regional towns as 'bidding war' heats up' (Australian Broadcasting Commission at https://www.abc.net. au/news/2025-01-22/gp-shortages-sting-regional-towns-as-bidding-war-heats-up/104848612 Accessed: 23rd January 2025).

We also find that elections tend to bring out some idiosyncratic aspects of rural life, and we offer a story about the way in which international backpackers, who are now a recognised feature of many rural communities, came together to 'save' a building – previously a church – that was falling into ruin. Many country towns rely on backpackers as casual staff to work in cafes, pubs, farms, and other small businesses. Many stay for several months, connect with the community, and contribute in many other ways outside the job. This story relates how a young woman from Bolivia began a campaign to clean up an old church building and restart church services after more than a decade. The church now attracts up to 50 people each Sunday, many coming for the social connection in the town of just over 400 residents.

'Backpackers restart Karumba church helping people to connect and make friends'(Australian Broadcasting Commission at https://www.abc.net.au/news/2025-02-16/backpackers-revive-outback-church-karumba/104890232 Accessed: 16th February 2025).

As a way of highlighting the power of FiFo and DiDo, we read a story about the community of Gracemere in Central Queensland, which, over the past two decades, has become an extensive satellite suburb, housing people who travel several hours out further west to the mines, as well as those unable to afford housing costs in cities. The story features how Gracemere is now in the top 10 of Queensland suburbs, but how business investment has not kept pace with the population growth.

'Rural Town Gracemere in top 10 list of Queensland suburbs' (Australian Broadcasting Commission at https://www.abc.net.au/news/2025-02-08/gracemere-qld-top-10-suburb-list-rents-soar-housing-unaffordable/104904146 Accessed: 8th February 2025).

We were heartened to read of a number of young allied health graduates choosing to take up positions in Mount Isa, 900 kms from the Queensland coast. Mt Isa has been a mining centre for many years and historically has had great difficulty attracting professionals. The successful recruitment strategy is largely due to a project establishing student placements via a university-sponsored health campus in Mt Isa. Several pharmacy and occupational therapy students undertaking internships as part of their studies found they liked the lifestyle and were later employed at the local hospital. 'Healthcare students relocate to outback Qld for Mt Isa hospital pharmacy internship' (Australian Broadcasting Commission at https://www.abc.net. au/news/2024-03-19/pharmacy-interns-fill-health-gap-in-outb ack/103599912 Accessed: 12th January 2025).

Climate change is a foundational experience for rural Australia, and climate variability is a factor in far NW Western Australia and FNQ. We found a recent (in the current Australian summer) story of Gasgoyne Junction, some 945 kms from Perth on the edge of the Western Desert, which experienced three days of extreme temperatures and was the hottest day in the world, on 3rd Feb 2025 at 49.2 degrees C (102.56 F). We note how the locals, who are used to hot weather, found this extreme and dangerous.

'Too hot to go for a swim: WA town endures three days at 49 degrees C' (Sharwood, 2025).

Our final story is one which is also a regular feature of any reporting on rural and remote Australia: the closure of infrastructure, in this case, the local pub. In many communities, the pub remains its heart and centre. It offers conviviality and community, it hosts visitors, and it provides shelter in hot weather. We read that there are more than a dozen currently for sale in Queensland, and this is probably reflected in Western Australia and perhaps other states. The buying, maintaining, and owning of a hotel used to be of high status. These days, it is not. One of these hotels is in Barcaldine, a town we discussed in Chapter 3.

'More than a dozen outback Queensland pubs for sale' (Australian Broadcasting Commission at https://www.abc.net.au/news/ 2025-02-19/more-than-a-dozen-outback-queensland-pubs-for-sale/104924746 Accessed: 19th February 2025).

As well as reading news items about life in rural and remote communities, travelling through outback towns and settlements also brings a multitude of stories about rural life and people. Rural Australia is certainly not homogeneous.

We end here on a more positive and humorous note.

Changes can also be reflected in a recent example of attachment to the rural more as an aspiration or search for an idea that comes to mind. On a recent visit to a small outpost town in South Australia, I met a young pilot who worked as a crop duster and as a helicopter pilot doing cattle mustering. I was intrigued by him describing how smart young women from the cities would descend on the town during the annual country race meeting and dance looking for prospective partners. The local eligible bachelors were very conscious of being scrutinised - did they drive a suitable 4 Wheel Drive, wear the RM Williams boots, etc.? The young men called these women 'acre-chasers'. They left the city on a search for a new and very different life on large cattle stations (ranches) with a suitable husband (Lesley).

4 A final note

This chapter provides a conclusion to our book and offers a seven-step journey towards working and living in rural Australia as a practicing social worker. We review the previous five chapters, and we offer a brief pastiche of life in the bush as we currently write this.

We hope that you found this book both interesting and useful. We wish you every success in your social work career and in whatever people and places you find yourself.

Reflection from your experience

You are a new social work graduate and have applied for your first social work position in a small rural town. You have just been advised that you have been shortlisted for an interview. The panel has asked that you present your practice framework at the interview and discuss how you would apply it in this job.

Using the schema below, record your thoughts and reflections against the elements and questions.

What is a practice framework?

A practice framework provides a foundation for one's practice. It is consistent with the values, purpose, and ethics of social work and combines the key components for practice – knowledge,

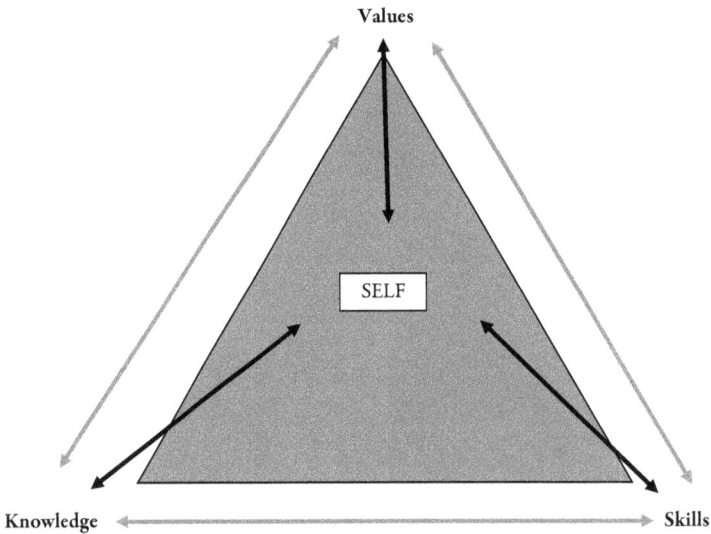

(Adapted from Chenoweth & McAuliffe, 2021)

FIG 6.1

(Adapted from Chenoweth & McAuliffe, 2021)

values, skills, and the use of self. Your framework should transcend the requirements of your employer organisation. Rather, it evolves and adapts over time, guiding your practice as you gain experience, work in different contexts, and acquire new knowledge and skills. Critical reflection is key to this process.

The core questions are:

What do I value?
What do I know?
What skills do I have?
How congruent are all of these with the way I am in the world and in my practice?
Who do I know who can help me? What materials do I have or can I access that can assist?

An example of a rural practice framework.

References

Alberta College of Social Workers (2019) Honouring Sacred Relationships: Wise Practices in Indigenous Social Work. February. https://www.acsw.ab.ca Accessed: 13th January, 2025.

Alker, J., Osorio, A. & Edwin, P. (2025) Medicaid's Role in Small Towns and Rural Areas. https://ccf.georgetown.edu/format/ research-reports/ January 15th. Accessed: 6th February, 2025.

Alston, A., Hazeleger, R. & Hargreaves, D. (2019). Social Work and Disasters: A Handbook for Practice. London: Routledge.

Ardoin, N. M. (2006). Toward an Interdisciplinary Understanding of Place: Lessons for Environmental Education. Canadian Journal of Environmental Education, 11, pp. 112–126.

Australian Association of Social Work (2025) Practice Standards. https://www.aasw.asn.au/ Accessed: 13th January, 2025.

Australian Broadcasting Commission (2025) Backpackers restart Karumba church helping people to connect and make friends. https://www.abc.net.au/news/2025-02-16/backpackers-revive-outback-church-karumba/104890232 Accessed: 16th February, 2025.

Australian Broadcasting Commission (2025) GP shortages sting regional towns as 'bidding war' heats up. https://www.abc.net.au/news/2025-01-22/gp-shortages-sting-regional-towns-as-bidding-war-heats-up/104848612 Accessed: 23rd January, 2025.

Australian Broadcasting Commission (2025) Healthcare students relocate to outback Qld for Mt Isa hospital pharmacy internship. https://www.abc.net.au/news/2024-03-19/pharmacy-interns-fill-health-gap-in-outback/103599912 Accessed: 12th January, 2025.

Australian Broadcasting Commission (2025) More than a dozen outback Queensland pubs for sale. https://www.abc.net.au/news/2025-02-19/more-than-a-dozen-outback-queensland-pubs-for-sale/104924746 Accessed: 19th February, 2025.

Australian Broadcasting Commission (2025) Rural town Gracemere in top 10 list of Queensland suburbs. https://www.abc.net.au/news/2025-02-08/gracemere-qld-top-10-suburb-list-rents-soar-housing-unaffordable/104904146 (Accessed: 8th February, 2025).

Australian Bureau of Statistics (2025) https://www.abs.gov.au Accessed: 22nd December, 2024.

Australian Government Department of Social Services (2025) Stronger Places, Stronger People https://www.dss.gov.au/stronger-places-stronger-people Accessed: 24th February, 2025.

Australian Government House of Representatives (2013) Cancer of the bush or salvation for our cities. Fly-in, fly-out and drive-in, drive-out workforce practices in Regional Australia. Standing Committee on Regional Australia. February. Canberra. https://www.aph.gov.au/parliamentary_business/committees/house_of_representatives_committees?url=ra/fifodido/report.htm Accessed: 24th November, 2024.

Australian Government National Disability Insurance Scheme (2025) Data Research. (https://dataresearch.ndis.gov.au Accessed: 8th February, 2025.

Australian Government Productivity Commission (1995) Charitable Organisations In Australia. https://www.pc.gov.au/inquiries/completed/charity Accessed: 15th December, 2024.

Australian Institute of Family Studies (2024). Facts and Figures. https://aifs.gov.au/research/facts-and-figures/families-and-family-composition Accessed: 3rd December, 2024.

Australian Institute of Health and Welfare (2024) Health Performance Framework. 1.15 Ear Health. https://www.indigenousshpf.gov.au/measures/1-15-ear-health Accessed: 24th November, 2024.

Australian Institute of Health and Welfare (2024) Profile of First Nations People. https://www.aihw.gov.au/reports/australias-welfare/profile-of-indigenous-australians Accessed: 9th February, 2025.

Baxter, J. (2011). Families in regional, rural and remote Australia. Melbourne: Australian Institute of Family Studies.

Bell, C. & Newby, H. (1972) Community Studies: An Introduction to the Sociology of the Local Community. London: Allen & Unwin.

Benevolent Society (2025) https://www.benevolent.org.au Accessed: 20th October, 2024.

Bennett, B. & Morse, C. (2023). The Continuous Improvement Cultural Responsiveness Tools (CICRT): Creating More Culturally Responsive Social Workers, Australian Social Work, 76, (3), pp. 315–329.

Bennett, B., Zubrzycki J. & Bacon, V. (2011). What Do We Know? The Experiences of Social Workers Working Alongside Aboriginal People, Australian Social Work, 64, (1), pp. 20–37.

Bowden, R (1995). Women of the Land. Stories of Australia's Rural Women. Sydney: ABC Books.

Bourke, L. & Lockie, S. (2001). 'Introduction' in L. Bourke & S. Lockie (eds) Rurality Bites. The Social and Environmental Transformation of Rural Australia, Annandale, NSW: Pluto Press. pp. 1–13.

Burghardt, S. (1982). Organizing for Community Action. Beverly Hills, CA.: Sage.

Canadian Association of Social Workers (2025) Code of Ethics and Scope of Practice. https://www.casw-acts.ca/en Accessed: 13th January, 2025.

Canadian Encyclopedia (2019) Hutterites in Canada. https://www.thecanadianencyclopedia.ca/en/article/hutterites Accessed: 2nd January, 2025.

Casey, E. S. (2001) Between Geography and Philosophy: What Does It Mean to Be in the Place-World? Annals of the Association of American Geographers, 91, (4). pp. 683–693.

Cheers, B. (1998). Welfare bushed: Social care in rural Australia. Aldershot, UK: Ashgate.

Chenoweth, L. (2004). 'Towards an integrative education for rural practice' Rural Society, 14, (3). pp. 276–287.

Chenoweth, L. & McAuliffe, D. (2021). The Road to social work and human service practice. 6th ed. South Melbourne: Cengage.

Chenoweth, L. & Stehlik, D. (1999). 'Interpreting Human Service Policy in Regional and Rural Queensland: the Practitioners' Perspective', Just Policy, 15. pp. 21–28.

Chenoweth, L. & Stehlik, D. (2001). Building resilient communities: Social work practice and rural Queensland. Australian Social Work, 54, (2). pp. 47–54.

Chenoweth, L. & Stehlik, D. (2002). 'Using technology in rural practice – Local Area Coordination in rural Australia', Rural Social Work, 7, (1). pp. 14 – 21.

Churchman, D. (2005). Safeguarding academic communities: retaining texture and passion in the academy. In T. Stehlik & P. Carden (eds).Beyond Communities of practice: theory as experience. Flaxton, Qld: Post Pressed. pp. 11–30.

Clapton, J (2008) 'Care": Moral concept or merely an organisational suffix? Journal of Intellectual Disability Research, 52, (7), pp. 1365–2788.

Cloke, P. (2006). 'Conceptualizing Rurality' In The Handbook of Rural Studies. London: Sage.

Collier, K. (1993). Social Work with Rural Peoples, (2nd ed). Vancouver: New Star Books.

Cooper, D. (1994). Productive, Relational and Everywhere? Conceptualising Power and Resistance within Foucauldian Feminism. Sociology 28(2), pp.435–454.

Cooperative Research Centre for Remote Economic Participation (2012). Fact Sheet About Remote Australia. https://www.ninti one.com.au/about-us/ Accessed: 18th June, 2013.

Cuomo, C. J. (1998). Feminism and Ecological Communities. An Ethic of Flourishing. London: Routledge.

Dale-Hallett, L. Diffey, R. O'Keefe, Q. & Wilson, K. (2008). 'Rural women reclaiming their place through symbols, stories and rituals'. In F. Vanclay, M. Higgins & A. Blacksaw (eds). Making Sense of Place. Exploring concepts and expressions of place through different senses and lenses, Canberra: National Museum of Australia Press. pp. 37–45.

Daley, M. (2021). Rural social work in the 21st century Serving individuals, families and communities in the countryside. 2nd ed. New York: Oxford University Press.

Daley, M. & Avant, F. (2013). Down-home social work: A strengths-based model for rural practice. In Scales, L., Streeter, C. & Cooper, S. (eds). Rural Social Work: Conceptual and historical foundations of rural social welfare. pp. 6–17. New York: Wiley.

Dominelli, L. (2012) Green social work: from environmental crises to environmental justice. Cambridge: Polity Press.

Ewing, B. (2008). Discourse and the construction of identity in a community of learning and a community of practice. In T. Stehlik & P. Carden (eds.), Beyond communities of practice: theory as experience Flaxton, Queensland: Post Pressed, pp. 149–170.

Frank, F. (2025). Personal communication. Common Ground Consulting, Meacham, Saskatchewan, Canada.

Frank, F. & Smith, A. (2006). Community Development and Partnerships. Perth: Curtin University of Technology.

Gammage, B. (2011). The Biggest Estate on Earth. How Aborigines made Australia. Sydney: Allen & Unwin.

Gasker, J. (2023). Generalist social work. Los Angeles, CA: Sage.

Goffman, E. (1963). Stigma. Notes on the Management of Spoiled Identity. New York: Simon & Schuster.

Government of Queensland (2024) Truth Telling & Healing Inquiry (2025) https://www.truth-telling-qld.com.au/final-statement-truth-telling-and-healing-inquiry Accessed: 28th January 2025.

Government of South Australia. (2016) Nuclear Fuel Cycle Royal Commission Report. Adelaide. May.

Gray, M. Coates, J. & Hetherington, T. (2013). Environmental Social Work. Abington, UK: Routledge.

Gray, S. (2020) The Northern Territory Intervention: An Evaluation. Castan Centre for Human Rights Law. Melbourne: Monash University.

Green, R. (2003). 'Social Work in Rural Areas: A Personal and Professional Challenge', Australian Social Work, 56, (3). pp. 209–219.

Haynes, K. S. & Mickelson, J. S. (1997). Affecting Change. Social Workers in the Political Arena. New York: Longman.

Howard. A., Katrak, M., Blakemore, T & Pallas, P. (2016) Rural, Regional and Remote Social Work: Practice Research from Australia. London: Routledge.

Jervis-Tracey, P, Chenoweth, L, McAuliffe, D., Stehlik, D. & O'Connor, B. (2012). Managing tensions in statutory professional practice: living and working in rural and remote communities. Australian and International Journal of Rural Education, 22, (2). pp. 97–112.

Jervis-Tracey, P., McAuliffe, D., Klieve, H., Chenoweth, L., O'Connor, B. & Stehlik, D. (2016). 'Negotiated policy spaces: Identifying tensions for rural professions in delivering their statutory responsibilities'. Journal of Rural Studies, 45, pp. 123–133.

Jones, W. R., Cheever, J. & Ficklin, J. (1971). Finding Community. A Guide to Community Research and Action. Cupertino, CA: J. E. Freel & Associates.

Kemmis, D. (1990). Community and the politics of place. Oklahoma City: University of Oklahoma Press.

Kordic, M., Shackleton, J. & Bidstrup, E. (2025). Regional WA leaders say detail critical amid housing promises. https://www.abc. net.au/news/2025-01-17/labor-opposition-pre-election-hous ing-promise-supply-demand-wa/104816126.   17th   January. Accessed 20th January 2025.

Korff, J (2020) Maralinga: How British Nuclear tests changed history forever. https://www.creativespirits.info/aboriginalculture/ history/maralinga-how-british-nuclear-tests-changed-history-forever Accessed: 12th December 2024.

Krieg Mayer, A. G. (2001). 'Rural social work: The perceptions and experiences of five remote practitioners', Australian Social Work, 54, (1). pp. 91–10.

Lathouras, A. (2016) A critical approach to citizen-led social work: Putting the political back into community development practice. Social Alternatives, 35, (4) pp. 32–36.

Lawrence, G. & Stehlik, D. (1996). 'A Direction towards sustainability? Australian Regional Communities and care for the aged' Journal of the International Community Development Society. 27, (1). pp. 45–55.

Lawrence, J. (1965). Professional social work in Australia. Canberra: Australian National University.

Lawson, H. A. (2016). Categories, Boundaries, and Bridges: The Social Geography of Schooling and the Need for New Institutional Designs. Educ.Sci. 6, (32). pp. 1–14.

Leonard, P. (1997). Postmodern welfare: Reconstructing an emancipatory project. London: Sage.

Lockie, S & Bourke, L (eds) (2001) Rurality Bites. The Social and Environmental Transformation of Rural Australia. Annandale, NSW: Pluto Press.

Lynch, D., Forde, C. & Lathouras, A. (2020). Changing contexts of practice: Challenges for social work and community development. Australian Social Work, 73, (2). pp. 245–253.

Maidment, J. & Bay, U. (2012) Rural practice: an agenda for the future. In J. Maidment & U. Bay (eds.) Social Work in Rural Australia. Enabling practice. pp. 221–234. Sydney: Allen & Unwin.

Martinez-Brawley, E.E. (1990). Perspectives on the Small Community. Humanistic Views for Practitioners, Washington, DC: NASW Press.

Martinez-Brawley, E.E. (2000). Close to home: human services in the small community. Washington, D.C.: NASW Press.

McAuliffe, D. (2005). 'I'm still standing: Impacts and consequences of ethical dilemmas for social workers in direct practice', Journal of Social Work Values and Ethics 2, (1). pp. 43–66.

McAuliffe, D., Chenoweth, L. & Stehlik, D. (2007). Rural practitioners of the future: Views of graduating students about rural child and family practice. Rural Social Work and Community Practice, 12, (1). pp. 6–14.

McLeish, K. (2017) Child Protection staff to be embedded with Queensland Police. https://www.abc.net.au/news/2017-07-24/child-safety-staff-embedded-queensland-police-at-risk-kids/8739108?utm_source=abc_news_app&utm_medium=content_shared&utm_campaign=abc_news_app&utm_content=mail Accessed: 24th November, 2024.

Monmonier, M. (1996). 2nd ed. How to Lie with Maps. University of Chicago Press, Chicago.

Montgomery, J. (2003). The issues shared by professionals living and working in rural communities in British Columbia. Canadian Journal of Rural Medicine. 8, (4). pp. 255–260.

Murphy, P. (2002). 'Sea Change: Re-Inventing Rural and Regional Australia' Transformations. (2). March.

Nakamura, G. & Walsh, H. (2024) Once bustling country towns losing people as industries, youth move away https://apple.new/AfNu3TAL1Rw2bl-HylsuH8g Accessed: 13th November, 2024.

National Association of Social Workers (2025) https://www.social workers.org/ Accessed: 13th January, 2025.

National Mental Health Pathways to Practice. (2025). https://www.apna.asn.au/education/national-mental-health-pathways-to-practice Accessed: 11th February, 2025.

National Rural Health Alliance. (2013). Use of 'fly-in fly-out' (FiFo) workforce practices in regional Australia. Submission #152 to House of Representatives Standing Committee on Regional Australia. Cancer of the bush or salvation for our cities? Fly-in, fly-out and drive-in, drive-out workforce practices in Regional Australia. 17th November.

O'Brien, F., Hawthorne-Steele, I., Pascoe, K.M., Moreland, R., Cownie, E & Killick, C. (2024) Bridging the gap between social work and community development: implementing a postgraduate training partnership. International Journal of Social Work Education, 43, (8). pp. 2218 2235.

Pascoe, B. (2014). Dark Emu: Black Seeds: Agriculture or Accident? Broome, Western Australia: Magabala Books.

Pattoni, L. (2012). Strengths-based approaches for working with individuals. Insight, 16. https://www.iriss.org.uk/resources/insights/strengths-based-appraoches-working-individuals. Accessed: 20th December, 2024.

Plank, D. N. (1996). 'Dreams of Community'. Politics of Education Association Year Book, pp. 13–20.

Plant, R., Lesser, H. & Taylor-Grooby, P. (1980). Political philosophy and social welfare. Essays on the normative basis of welfare provision. London: Routledge & Kegan Paul.

Prehn, J. (2024). An Indigenous Strengths-based Theoretical Framework, Australian Social Work, 22ndMay. DOI: 10.1080/0312407X.2024.2340464 Accessed: 9th February, 2025.

Pugh, R. (2003). 'Considering the Countryside: Is There a Case for Rural Social Work?' British Journal of Social Work, 33, (1). pp. 67–85.

Pugh, R. (2007). 'Dual Relationships: Personal and Professional Boundaries in Rural Social Work' British Journal of Social Work, 37, (3). pp. 1405–1423.

Pugh, R. & Cheers, B. (2010). Rural social work: an international perspective. Bristol: Policy Press.

Queensland Council of Social Service (2019). Place-based approaches for community change QCOSS' guide and toolkit. https://www.qcoss.org.au/contents-page-for-place-based-approach-and-toolkit/ Accessed: 2nd February, 2025.

Ramsay, S. & Boddy, J. (2017). Environmental social work: A conceptual analysis. The British Journal of Social Work, 47, pp. 68–86.

Read, P. (1996). Returning to Nothing. The meaning of lost places. Melbourne: Cambridge University Press.

Rein, M. (1970). Social Work in Search of a Radical Profession. Social Work. Journal of the National Association of Social Workers, 15, (2). pp. 13–28.

Remote Australians Matter. (2024) August 15. https://www.remoteaustraliansmatter.org Accessed: 2nd December, 2024.

Rich, J., Booth, A., Reddy P. & Rowlands, A. (2014). The Step by Step Bushfire Support Service Qualitative Evaluation Report. Centre for Rural and Remote Mental Health, Newcastle, NSW: University of Newcastle.

Ricketts, T. (2005). Workforce issues in rural areas: A focus on policy equity. American Journal of Public Health, 95, (1). pp. 42–48.

Rousseau, N. (1995) What is rurality? Occasional Papers R. Coll. Gen. Prac. (71) September. pp. 1 -4. www.ncbi.nlm.nih.gov Accessed: 21st September, 2017.

Royal Flying Doctor Service (2024) https://www.flyingdoctor.org. au/about-the-rfds/history/ Accessed: 12th November, 2024.)

Saleebey, D. (Ed.). (2013). The strengths perspective in social work practice. (6th Ed.) Pearson.

Sargent, M. (1995). The New Sociology for Australians. Melbourne: Longman. 3rd ed.

Sharwood, A (2025) Too hot to go for a swim: WA town endures three days at 49 degrees C. Weatherzone News. https://www. weatherzone.com.au/news/too-hot-to-go-for-a-swim-wa-town-endures-three-days-of-49c/1890344   Accessed: 7th February, 2025.

Shaw, M. (2008). Community development and the politics of community. Community Development Journal, 43, (1), pp. 24–36.

Simmerton, J. (2025) Dire warning amid rural Queensland health-care exodus. The Courier Mail. 24th January. https://www.cour iermail.com.au/news/queensland/dire-warning-amid-rural-que ensland-healthcare-exodus/news-story/a97370f51cd4698cf 553c8da9321aa4b#:~:text=Picture%3A%20Russell%20Shakespe are.-,Rural%20Queensland%20is%20losing%20healthcare%20 workers%20at%20a%20frightening%20rate,needs%20to%20 happen%20by%202032 Accessed: 24th February, 2025.

Stehlik, D. (2001). 'Out there': Spaces, places and border cross-ings. In S Lockie and L Bourke (eds.) Rurality Bites. The social and environmental transformation of rural Australia. Annandale, NSW:Pluto Press. pp. 31– 41.

Stehlik, D. (2013). 'Social work practice in drought: An Australian case study'. In M. Gray, J. Coates & T. Hetherington (eds) Environmental Social Work. London: Taylor & Francis, pp. 135–154.

Stehlik, D. (2017). 'Rurality, disability and place identity' In K Soldatic & K Johnson eds, Disability and Rurality. Identity, Gender and Belonging London: Routledge. pp. 69–80.

Stehlik, D. & Chenoweth, L. (2005). 'Collaboration/Participation/ Friendship: Formative Evaluation as 'Praxis''. Australian Journal of Qualitative Research. 5, (1), pp. 41–49.

Stehlik, T. (2018). Educational Philosophy for 21st Century Teachers. Cham, Switzerland: Palgrave MacMillan.

Stehlik, T. & Carden, P. (eds) (2005). Beyond communities of practice: theory as experience. Flaxton, Queensland: Post Pressed.

Stewart, B.J. and Allan, J. (2013). Building Relationships with Aboriginal People: A Cultural Mapping Toolbox, Australian Social Work, 66(1), pp. 118–129.

Tilbury, T., Aitchison, R., Chenoweth, L., McAuliffe, D,, Stehlik, D. & Osmond, J. (2014). 'Valuing Local Knowledge in Child Protection Practice' Communities, Children and Families Australia 8, (1), pp. 5–20.

Tomaney, J (2013) Parochialism – a defence. Progress in Human Geography, Vol 37, No. 5 https://journals.sagepub.com/doi/ 10.1177/0309132512471235 Accessed: 27th January, 2025.

Trotter, C., Rooney, R. & Dewberry Rooney, G. (2020). 'Strategies for Work with Involuntary Clients', Australian Social Work, 73, (3), pp. 263–266.

Turbett, C. & Pye, J. (eds) (2024). Rural Social Work in the UK. Themes and Challenges for the Future. London: Palgrave Macmillan.

Vanclay, F. (2008). 'Place matters' In F Vanclay, M Higgins & A Blacksaw (eds). Making Sense of Place. Exploring concepts and expressions of place through different senses and lenses. Canberra: National Museum of Australia Press, pp. 3–11.

Warr, D., Luscombe, G. & Couch, D. (2021). 'Hype, evidence gaps and digital divides: Telehealth blind spots in rural Australia'.

Health: An Interdisciplinary Journal for the Social Study of Health Illness and Medicine 27, (4) https://journals.sagepub.com/doi/abs/10.1177/13634593211060763. Accessed: 10th January, 2025.

Wedesweiler, M (2025) 'Second-class citizens": the 'grim' reality of avoidable deaths in regional Australia. https://www.sbs.com.au/news/article/second-class-citizens-the-grim-reality-of-avoidable-deaths-in-regional-australia/s5cylskf8 Accessed: 22nd February, 2025.

Westoby, P & Shevallar, L (2016) (eds), Learning and Mobilising for Community Development. London: Routledge.

Winter, I. (ed) (2000). Social Capital and public policy in Australia, Melbourne: Australian Institute of Family Studies.

Wright Mills, C. (1970). The Sociological Imagination. Harmondsworth: Penguin.

Index

www.ingramcontent.com/pod-product-compliance
Lightning Source LLC
Chambersburg PA
CBHW070332270326
41926CB00017B/3847